ADVANCED SOFTWARE ENGINEERING: EXPANDING THE FRONTIERS OF SOFTWARE TECHNOLOGY

IFIP – The International Federation for Information Processing

IFIP was founded in 1960 under the auspices of UNESCO, following the First World Computer Congress held in Paris the previous year. An umbrella organization for societies working in information processing, IFIP's aim is two-fold: to support information processing within its member countries and to encourage technology transfer to developing nations. As its mission statement clearly states,

> IFIP's mission is to be the leading, truly international, apolitical organization which encourages and assists in the development, exploitation and application of information technology for the benefit of all people.

IFIP is a non-profitmaking organization, run almost solely by 2500 volunteers. It operates through a number of technical committees, which organize events and publications. IFIP's events range from an international congress to local seminars, but the most important are:

• The IFIP World Computer Congress, held every second year;
• Open conferences;
• Working conferences.

The flagship event is the IFIP World Computer Congress, at which both invited and contributed papers are presented. Contributed papers are rigorously refereed and the rejection rate is high.

As with the Congress, participation in the open conferences is open to all and papers may be invited or submitted. Again, submitted papers are stringently refereed.

The working conferences are structured differently. They are usually run by a working group and attendance is small and by invitation only. Their purpose is to create an atmosphere conducive to innovation and development. Refereeing is less rigorous and papers are subjected to extensive group discussion.

Publications arising from IFIP events vary. The papers presented at the IFIP World Computer Congress and at open conferences are published as conference proceedings, while the results of the working conferences are often published as collections of selected and edited papers.

Any national society whose primary activity is in information may apply to become a full member of IFIP, although full membership is restricted to one society per country. Full members are entitled to vote at the annual General Assembly, National societies preferring a less committed involvement may apply for associate or corresponding membership. Associate members enjoy the same benefits as full members, but without voting rights. Corresponding members are not represented in IFIP bodies. Affiliated membership is open to non-national societies, and individual and honorary membership schemes are also offered.

ADVANCED SOFTWARE ENGINEERING: EXPANDING THE FRONTIERS OF SOFTWARE TECHNOLOGY

IFIP 19th World Computer Congress, First International Workshop on Advanced Software Engineering, August 25, 2006, Santiago, Chile

Edited by

Sergio F. Ochoa
Department of Computer Science
Universidad de Chile
Santiago, Chile

Gruia-Catalin Roman
Department of Computer Science and Engineering
Washington University in St. Louis
St. Louis, Missouri, USA

 Springer

Advanced Software Engineering: Expanding the Frontiers of Software Technology

Edited by S. Ochoa and G. Roman

    p. cm. (IFIP International Federation for Information Processing, a Springer Series in Computer Science)

ISSN: 1571-5736 / 1861-2288 (Internet)

ISBN: 13: 978-1-4419-4194-7   eISBN: 10: 0-387-34831-X
Printed on acid-free paper
e-ISBN: 13: 978-0-387-34831-5

9 8 7 6 5 4 3 2 1
springer.com

Preface

On behalf of the Organizing Committee for this event, we are glad to welcome you to IWASE 2006, the First International Workshop on Advanced Software Engineering. We hope you will enjoy the traditional Chilean hospitality and, of course, please tell us how we can make your visit a pleasant and useful experience.

The goal of this Workshop is to create a new forum for researchers, professionals and educators to discuss advanced software engineering topics. A distinctive feature of this Workshop is its attempt to foster interactions between the Latin-American software engineering community and computer scientists around the world. This is an opportunity to discuss with other researchers or simply to meet new colleagues. IWASE 2006 has been organized to facilitate strong interactions among those attending it and to offer ample time for discussing each paper.

IWASE 2006 attracted 28 submissions from 14 countries, 8 of them outside Latin-America. Each of the 28 articles was reviewed by at least three members of the Program Committee. As a result of this rigorous reviewing process, 13 papers were accepted: nine full papers and four work-in-progress papers. These papers were grouped in four tracks: software architecture, software modeling, software development process and experiences in software development.

Several people have worked in the preparation of the event. We would like to thank Hernán Astudillo, Cecilia Bastarrica, Yadran Eterovic, Andrés Neyem and Marcela Varas for their enthusiastic support and hard work as members of the Organizing Committee. We want to thank John Atkinson, Ramón Puigjaner and Mauricio Solar for the support to this workshop. Also, we are grateful to the student volunteers whom have helped with many details. We wish to mention two institutions and a company which aided to make this event possible. The institutions are Universidad de Chile and Washington University in St. Louis, which provided their support. The company supporting this event is Microsoft Chile.

Please get involved!

Sergio F. Ochoa
Gruia-Catalin Roman
Conference Chairs, IWASE 2006

Program Committee

Bernhard K. Aichernig, TU Graz, (Austria)
Roberto Aldunate, University of Illinois at Urbana-Champaign (USA)
Pedro Antunes, University of Lisboa (Portugal)
Hernán Astudillo, Universidad Técnica Federico Santa María (Chile)
Felix Bachmann, Carnegie Mellon University (USA)
Doo-Hwan Bae, KAIST, (South Korea).
Federico Balaguer, University of Illinois at Urbana-Champaign (USA)
Cecilia Bastarrica, Universidad de Chile (Chile)
Marcos Borges, Universidade Federal do Rio de Janeiro (Brazil)
Mariano Cilia, Darmstadt University of Technology (Germany)
Yadran Eterovic, Pontificia Universidad Católica de Chile (Chile)
Jesús Favela, CICESE (Mexico)
Eduardo Fernández, Florida Atlantic University (USA)
George Fernández, RMIT University (Australia)
Cristina Gacek, University of Newcastle (England)
Alejandra Garrido, University of Illinois at Urbana-Champaign (USA)
Luis A. Guerrero, Universidad de Chile (Chile)
Claudia Marcos, UNICEN (Argentina)
Gabriel Moreno, Carnegie Mellon University (USA)
Jaime Navón, Pontificia Universidad Católica de Chile (Chile)
Mario Piattini, Universidad de Castilla - La Mancha (Spain)
Claudia Pons, Universidad Nacional de La Plata (Argentina)
Karl Reed, La Trobe University (Australia)
Guilherme H. Travassos, Universidade Federal do Rio de Janeiro (Brazil)
Hongji Yang, De Montfort University (England)
Marcela Varas, Universidad de Concepción (Chile)
Marcello Visconti, Universidad Técnica Federico Santa María (Chile)

Organizing Committee

Hernán Astudillo, Universidad Técnica Federico Santa María, (Chile).
Cecilia Bastarrica, Universidad de Chile, (Chile).
Yadran Eterovic, Pontificia Universidad Católica de Chile, (Chile).
Andrés Neyem, Universidad de Chile, (Chile).
Sergio F. Ochoa, Universidad de Chile, (Chile).
Marcela Varas, Universidad de Concepción, (Chile).

Table of Contents

Session 4: Experiences in Software Development

A Meshing Tool Product Line Architecture

María Cecilia Bastarrica[1], Nancy Hitschfeld-Kahler[1], Pedro O. Rossel[1,2]

[1] Computer Science Department, FCFM, Universidad de Chile
Blanco Encalada 2120, Santiago, Chile
[2] Departamento de Computación e Informática, Universidad Católica del Maule
Avenida San Miguel 3605, Talca, Chile
{cecilia|nancy|prossel}@dcc.uchile.cl

Abstract. Meshing tools are extremely complex pieces of software. Traditionally, they have been built in a one by one basis, without systematically reusing already developed parts. The area has matured so that we can currently think of building meshing tools in a more industrial manner. Software product lines is a trend in software development that promotes systematic reuse. We propose a layered product line architecture for meshing tools that can be instantiated with different algorithms, ways of implementing basic concepts, and even for two or three dimensional meshing tools. We specify it formally using xADL and we show that the architecture is compatible with a series of already built tools. This work is the beginning of a domain analysis that has the potential to go beyond the sometimes rigid descriptions provided by architectural description languages.

1 Introduction

Meshes are used for numerical modeling, visualizing and/or simulating objects or phenomena. A mesh is a discretization of a certain domain geometry. This discretization can be either composed by a unique type of element, such as triangles, tetrahedra or hexahedra, or a combination of different types of elements. Meshing tools generate and manage these discretizations.

Meshing tools are inherently sophisticated software due to the complexity of the concepts involved, the large number of interacting elements they manage, and the application domains where they are used. Meshing tools need to accomplish specific functionality while still having an acceptable performance. Managing thousands and even millions of elements with a reasonable use of computational resources –mainly processor time and storage– becomes a must if the tool is to be usable at all. Lately, however, other qualities related to modifiability have become relevant in meshing tool development.

There are many application domains where meshing tools are used, ranging from mechanics design to medicine [12]. Each domain requires slightly different functionality. For this reason, a variety of meshing tools have been built differing on the functionality included, the algorithms used for implementing their functionality, the way data is represented, or the format of the data used as input or

---

Please use the following format when citing this chapter:

Bastarrica, M.C., Hitschfeld-Kahler, N., Rossel, P.O., 2006, in IFIP International Federation for Information Processing, Volume 219, Advanced Software Engineering: Expanding the Frontiers of Software Technology, eds. Ochoa, S., Roman, G.-C., (Boston: Springer), pp. 1–15.

output. Also depending on the application domain, it may be required to have one, two or three dimensional meshes, each one maybe using different types of basic modeling elements. For example, analyzing the tree rings requires 2D meshes generated from an image, simulating tree growth uses surface meshes, and modeling brain shift during surgery requires 3D meshes.

Developing any complex software from scratch in a one by one basis is expensive, slow and error prone, but this is the way meshing tools have traditionally been built. If this development task is not performed in a systematic way using good software engineering practices, it may easily get out of control making it almost impossible to debug and even more difficult to modify. There have been some efforts lately applying software engineering concepts in meshing tool development, mainly building general purpose libraries that facilitate reuse. Also object-orientation and design patterns have the potential of enhancing software reuse at the code and design levels, and there is some experience in using these techniques for developing meshing tools.

The software architecture is one of the main artifacts developed during the software life cycle [15] because it determines most of the non-functional characteristics the resulting software will have, and it is also one of the most difficult documents to change once the software is deployed [2]. Architectural patterns [7] are used as guidelines for architectural design by reusing design knowledge at a high level of abstraction. Different architectural patterns promote different non-functional characteristics. In this way, for example, by using component and connector patterns such as client-server or repository, runtime properties can be modeled. Or using module patterns such as decomposition or layers, properties related to maintainability can be modeled [8].

Software product lines is a trend for planned massive reuse of software assets [9]. The most typical reusable assets are software components, but we can also reuse the product line architecture (PLA), software requirement documentation, and test cases, among others. The PLA is an important reusable asset because all software products in the family share the same design [6]. Therefore, the PLA design should be carefully approached making sure it will produce software that complies with the desired requirements.

In this paper we present the product line architecture for a family of meshing tools. Its design is based on the general architecture of published meshing products, as well as our own experience in building this type of tools. We intended to provide a PLA that would promote flexibility and extensibility, so that existing algorithms, data structures, data formats and visualizers could be combined in different ways to produce a variety of meshing tools appropriate for diverse application domains, sharing the software structure. The PLA is modeled following the layered architectural pattern [7]. This module view type is used for promoting modifiability, reusability and portability. Sometimes it is argued that layered architectures may penalize performance, but we have found that performance does not necessarily degrade significantly using the proposed PLA [19]. In [17] it is reported that a tool implementing this layered architecture performs almost as fast as TetGen [26], a widely used open source meshing tool.

We formally define the PLA using xADL 2.0, an XML-based ADL specially designed to support the description of architectures as explicit collections of components and connectors [18]. There are graphical tools that make it easier to specify software architectures using xADL. xADL has also shown to be appropriate to specify product lines architectures [10].

We show how the proposed PLA can be instantiated for generating different meshing tools. In particular we show how already implemented tools can be seen as instantiations of our product family, independently of the methods followed for generating the meshes and the dimensions of the managed mesh.

The paper is structured as follows. In Section 2 we present and discuss concepts such as software architecture and software product lines and how they have been used in the development of meshing tools. We also present some efforts in developing meshing tools. Section 3 presents the proposed layered architecture for our product family of meshing tools, and Section 4 shows a series of different instantiations of this PLA to produce different meshing tools. Finally, in Section 5 we present some conclusions and describe our work in progress.

2 Related Work

There is a variety of meshing tools developed for different purposes [25]. However, the use of software engineering principles in meshing tool design has spread only in the last five years. Some examples include the design of generic extensible geometry interfaces between CAD modelers and mesh generators [21,23,27,30], the design of object-oriented data structures and procedural classes for mesh generation [22], and the computational geometry algorithm library CGAL [14]. Also recently it was publish a discussion on the usage of formal methods for improving reliability of meshing software [13]. There have also been some attempts in using software product family concepts for building meshing tools [3,28].

Software product lines (SPL) is a modern approach towards software development based on planned massive reuse. The idea is to provide a reuse infrastructure that supports a family of products, and to spend the resources in such a way that a high return of investment and reduce time-to-market can be achieved [29]. All elements subject to reuse are called core assets of the SPL. So, an SPL is a set of products that are built using core assets in a planned manner and that satisfy the needs of a market segment [9]. One of the most important assets in a SPL is the product line architecture (PLA). Opportunistic reuse does not usually work [6]; thus, assets in a SPL should be developed in such a way that reuse is promoted. This development process is longer and more expensive than developing one product at a time, but if assets are reused enough times, it is still cost-effective. Experience has shown that the costs of developing reusable assets is paid off after the second or third product is built [33]. The strategy for building software product lines is to identify commonalities, variabilities and optional modules.

To our knowledge, SPL has neither been widely used as an approach for developing meshing tools, nor have architectural patterns been considered as a basis for designing any particular meshing tool architecture. Product line architectures must, by definition, be flexible to foster all products in the SPL, and promote modifiability so that variabilities could be incorporated. Therefore, it results natural to use module view type patterns [8], and more particularly a layered architectural pattern [7] as a guideline for designing the PLA.

There are several different architecture description languages (ADLs) [20], but not all of them are good for specifying PLAs.

In [5], an integrated notation for specifying software architectures in three levels of abstraction is proposed: structure, behavior and domain specific abstract data types. In [4] it is shown how to use this notation for defining a PLA. The notation helps in the process of identifying and localizing variations, but this it is not only non-standard for architecture specification, but also it has little tool support.

Koala is a software component model designed for creating software product lines for a large variety of products [31,32]. Koala handles variation using composition, where selection of reusable components is bound in different ways to obtain different products. Koala was specifically created for modeling embedded systems. Mae is a technique, along with a supporting toolset, to formally specify, analyze, and evolve software architectures. It uses xADL 2.0 as an extensible notation to model the PLA as we do. We may use Mae in the future to face other development stages.

UML has become a standard notation for documenting software design. With the new UML 2.0 standard, some modeling elements specifically for software architectures were incorporated, but there are still no primitives for documenting connectors or architectural styles. However, there have been some efforts to extend UML in order to be able to use it as an ADL [24]. To our knowledge, UML has not been widely used for defining PLA. xADL improves on the UML approach in two significant ways: features and extensibility. With respect to features, xADL 2.0's type system and product-line support are abilities not present in UML 2.0 [10].

3 Product Line Architecture

Independently of the application domain, any meshing tool may provide certain general functionality:

- read the domain geometry and physical values
- generate an initial mesh
- refine, derefine, improve or smooth a mesh according to a quality criterion within a specified region
- evaluate the quality of a resulting mesh
- store the mesh into a file possible with different formats
- visualize the mesh

The specification of the input geometry and the physical values can be generated by different CAD programs or by other mesh generation tools. That is why there should be a component in charge of managing input/output formats.

It may be required to follow different algorithms for generating an initial mesh. These algorithms receive the domain geometry, and generate a mesh that represents an initial discretization of the domain.

Modeling different problems may require different point distributions in the mesh, thus a variety of refinement strategies have been proposed. A refinement strategy consists of dividing coarse elements into smaller ones until a set of refinement criteria within a specified region is fulfilled. Improvement is a special kind of refinement where the quality of the mesh elements is improved, not necessarily dividing existing elements.

Smoothing and derefinement processes are also applied according to some criteria and over different domain regions. Smoothing moves point locations in order to improve the local quality of the mesh elements. And refinement is the inverse process of refinement, making the mesh coarser again.

The evaluation process lets the user know the real quality of the mesh, in terms of percentage of good and bad elements.

The tools that form part of the family may include some or all of these processes. The PLA determines the product line scope limiting what products can be built, but at the same time it should be flexible enough to allow designers to build all desired tools. Flexibility and interchangeability are two of the non-functional requirements that guide our PLA design; this is why we chose a module view type architecture, and more precisely a layered architecture.

Figure 1 shows the structure of the meshing tool PLA. This architecture is specified using ArchStudio [1]. For simplicity we only include the connectors between layers and not those among modules within a layer even though they exist and they may be quite complex. Table 1 includes a general description of each type of component included in the PLA shown in Fig. 1.

The architecture is composed by four layers: *User Interface*, *Algorithms*, *Model* and *Input Output*. In the *User Interface* layer there is only one module: *Selector*. The *Algorithms* contains the modules corresponding to all typical mesh processes. The *Model* layer includes the representation of all entities used

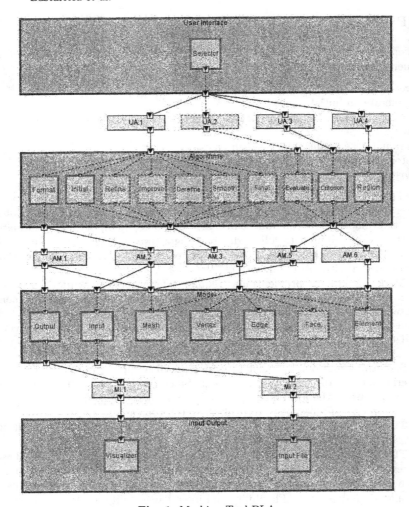

Fig. 1. Meshing Tool PLA

for modeling the mesh as well as the processes for input and output the corresponding data. Finally, in the *Input Output* layer there are modules for reading mesh data and/or visualizing it. In xADL, each layer is defined as a structure. Figure 2 shows the xADL specification of the complete *Meshing Tool* PLA. Figure 3 shows the xADL specification of the **Refine** module. This module is included in the *Algorithms* structure.

Refine and/or improve represent the core functionality of a meshing tool. In our PLA, both are presented as optional even though it may seem counter

Layer	Component Type	Description
User Interface	Selector	Menu for choosing the process to execute in the following step
Algorithms	Format	Translates the input geometry (domain) specified in any of the accepted formats in a normalized format
	Initial	Generates an initial mesh of the domain
	Refine	Divides the mesh elements that do not satisfy the refinement criterion in the specified region
	Improve	Improves the mesh quality by dividing or reorganizing its elements according to the criterion in the specified region
	Derefine	Eliminates mesh elements according to a criterion in the specified region
	Smooth	Improves the quality of the elements by moving mesh points according to some criterion in the specified region
	Final	Applies a post-process to the complete mesh
	Evaluate	Generates statistics of the current mesh according to a quality criterion
	Criterion	Represents a geometric or physical quality that an element must fulfill. For example, the minimum angle of each element must be greater than $25°$ and/or the maximum edge length must be less than 2
	Region	Represents the part of the domain where the selected algorithm is applied to any element that does not fulfill the specified criterion
Model	Output	Gets the domain discretization and physical attributes and stores it in the required format
	Mesh	Contains the discretization of the domain. It is composed of elements, faces (only in 3D), edges and vertices
	Vertex	Represents a point of the discretization
	Edge	Represents a connection between two vertices
	Face	Represents the connections on an element surface. A triangular face is the one defined by three vertices or edges, and a rectangular face is defined by four vertices or edges
	Element	Represents a discretization cell. It can be a triangle or rectangle in 2D, or a tetrahedron or an hexahedron, among others, in 3D
	Input	Reads the domain description in a specific format and stores it as part of the mesh
Input Output	Visualizer	Tool that allows the visualization of the domain discretization and physical attributes
	InputFile	Contains the domain description in a format generated by a CAD tool

Table 1. Component types

intuitive. Actually, at least one of them must be included in any tool instantiation. Though they represent different concepts, there are certain algorithms that perform both, so there are meshing tools that provide both functionalities only including one of them. There are other tools that prefer to use different algorithms for each one. This is why we give the opportunity of choosing different configurations. The `Face` module in the `Model` layer is also defined as optional. For all 3D tools there must exist a `Face` module, but it is meaningless for 2D tools.

```
+ <types:archStructure types:id="Meshing Tool"
        xsi:type="types:ArchStructure">
+ <types:archStructure types:id="User Interface"
        xsi:type="types:ArchStructure">
+ <types:archStructure types:id="Algorithms"
        xsi:type="types:ArchStructure">
+ <types:archStructure types:id="Model"
        xsi:type="types:ArchStructure">
+ <types:archStructure types:id="Input Output"
        xsi:type="types:ArchStructure">
```

Fig. 2. Structures used in Meshing Tool Architecture

As we can see in Figs. 1 and 3, `Refine` exposes two interfaces, called *Refine.Top* and *Refine.Bottom*, respectively. The former has the direction *in*, and the latter has the direction *out*; this means that this component can be used by any component in the upper layer, and `Refine` may use other modules contained in the lower layer, following the rules of the layered architectural pattern [7].

According to the graphical specification in Fig. 1 where `Refine` is defined as optional, the xADL includes the *options:optional* tag indicating optionality.

4 Product Instantiation

In order to show the consistency of the proposed PLA, we present some products that may be part of the SPL.

The process of designing meshing products using the proposed PLA has two stages: component type selection and implementation selection. First, the component types that are to be included must be chosen; here some of the optional component types may not be included. In the second stage, a particular implementation needs to be chosen for every selected component type. In this way, different meshing tools may differ in their functionality (component types included) or in their implementation (concrete component implementation assigned to each component type).

```
- <types:component types:id="Refine" xsi:type="types:Component">
    <types:description xsi:type="instance:Description">
        Refine module</types:description>
    - <types:interface types:id="Refine.Top" xsi:type="types:Interface">
        <types:description xsi:type="instance:Description">
            Top interface</types:description>
        <types:direction xsi:type="instance:Direction"> in</types:direction>
    </types:interface>
    - <types:interface types:id="Refine.Bottom" xsi:type="types:Interface">
        <types:description xsi:type="instance:Description">
            Bottom interface< /types:description>
        <types:direction xsi:type="instance:Direction"> out</types:direction>
    </types:interface>
    + <options:optional xsi:type="options:Optional">
</types:component>
```

Fig. 3. Refine Module Specification

Our SPL is oriented towards building tools for the generation of meshes required for numerically solving partial differential equations. The most widely used numerical methods for solving these equations are: finite differences, control volumes, and finite elements. Typically mesh generators have been implemented using Delaunay algorithms, octree or advancing front. Meshes satisfying the Delaunay condition are those that provide the most equilateral partition of a set of 2D points. Octrees and advancing front are specific techniques for mesh generation. In Section 4.1 we present tools for generating finite element meshes and in Section 4.2 we present control volume meshes; in each case we present one example for 2D meshes and another one for 3D meshes.

4.1 Finite Element Meshes

For a large range of problems using the finite element method, isotropic meshes are required. The isotropy is measured based on the geometrical properties of each mesh element, e.g. more equilateral elements are considered better than elements with too small or too large angles.

Simple 2D Triangulation Tool 2D triangulations require some of the component types identified as part of the Algorithms layer of the PLA in Fig. 3. In particular, a tool that generates Delaunay triangulations where all triangles have the minimum angle greater than a threshold value specified by the user, requires the component types described as part of Table 2. 2D triangulations do not require the Face component type, but all other component types in the Model layer must be included.

Component Type	Description
Selector	After generating the initial mesh, only the improvement algorithm can be selected letting the user to provide the minimum angle for the criterion to be applied
Initial	Delaunay_algorithm is used for generating the initial mesh
Improve	Delaunay_improvement_algorithm is used for improving
Criterion	Minimum_angle is used as a general criterion
Region	Whole_geometry is used as the region where the improvement algorithm is applied

Table 2. 2D triangulation meshing tool (taken from [3])

Even though the Format component type is not optional, in this case it has a dummy functionality since the mesh is already read in its required format.

3D Tetrahedral Meshes In Table 3 the algorithms included in a particular 3D finite element mesh generator taken from [19] are described. This meshing tool allows the generation of 3D Delaunay and non-Delaunay meshes with a user specified point density and element quality. It also understands different input and output data formats. All component types included in the Model layer must also be realized as part of the tool, including Face since it is a 3D tool.

Component Type	Description
Selector	After generating the initial mesh, the Refine and Improve components can be chosen several times
Initial	GMVDelaunay generates a Delaunay mesh
Format	Translates the Off and Mesh formats into the appropriate format understandable by the meshing tool using OffFormat and MeshFormat, respectively
Refine	LeppBisection refines generally according to the longest edge criterion, or any other refinement criterion
Improve	LeppDelaunay improves the mesh with the CircumRadiusEdgeRatio criterion, or any other improvement criterion
Criterion	A set of different eligible criteria for refinement and improvement; e.g. LongestEdge, CircumRadiusEdgeRatio, VolumeEdgeRatio
Region	Region where the algorithm is applied; e.g. WholeGeometry, Cube, Sphere

Table 3. 3D finite element mesh generator (taken from [19])

4.2 Control Volume Meshes

For the simulation of semiconductor devices using the control volume method, it is required to have anisotropic Delaunay conforming meshes where no part of a Voronoi region of an internal point is outside the domain [11]. In 2D, this requirement is fulfilled if there is no obtuse angle opposite to boundary/interface edges. In 3D, for each boundary face the center of the smallest circumsphere must be inside the domain. In addition, too large angles in the interior of the domain and too high vertex edge connectivity must be avoided.

2D Triangulations In [3], a tool for the simulation of semiconductor devices is described. Here the mesh is read already in the format the tool is able to understand, so the Format component is assumed to have a dummy functionality. This tool is essentially used for improving and post-processing a mesh already generated and refined by another meshing generator. The specific component types chosen and their particular implementations are those described in Table 4.

Component Type	Description
Selector	Allows to enter a specific improvement region and criterion, and also to choose the following algorithm to be applied (either Improve or Final)
Initial	Reads the already generated Delaunay mesh
Improve	Applies the Delaunay_improvement_algorithm to the specified region with a particular criterion
Final	Post-processes the mesh eliminating obtuse angles opposite to the boundary (Non_obtuse_boundary_algorithm)
Criterion	Improvement criteria such as Maximum_edge_vertex_connectivity and Maximum_angle
Region	Region where the improvement is applied; in the example only Whole_geometry is used, but it may also be Circle or Rectangle

Table 4. 2D control volume mesh (taken from [3])

3D Mixed Element Meshes A tool for 3D semiconductor simulation is described in [16]. In this case, the mesh is composed of different types of elements, i.e. cuboides, prisms, pyramids and tetrahedra. The implementation is based on a modified octree approach. Even though this application was not developed with the product line concepts in mind, it fits within the PLA structure with little effort. The components included as part of the tool are described in Table 5.

Component Type	Description
Selector	Allows to enter a list of criteria and their associated regions, and then the whole process is invoked
Initial	Reads the device geometry and generates a first coarse mixed element mesh (Fit_Device_Geometry)
Refine	Divides element in order to fit physical and geometric parameter values (Refine_Grid)
Final	Improves elements in order to fulfill the Voronoi region requirement and generates the final mixed element mesh (Make_Irregular_Leaves_Splittable)
Region	Regions where the refinement is applied, e.g. cuboid or rectangle, among others
Criterion	Doping_Difference and Longest_Edge as the main refinement criteria
Format	Outputs the mesh in a format understandable by the visualizer (Write_Geometrical_Information and Write_Doping_Information)

Table 5. 3D control volume mesh (taken from [16])

5 Conclusion

Meshing tool construction has not generally been approached using modern software engineering techniques, even though being sophisticated pieces of software makes them an appropriate application area.

The software product line approach intends to reuse all the artifacts that are built during software development in new products that fall within the SPL scope. The PLA is one of the most important assets in a SPL because it determines the non functional properties the resulting software will have. Having a well defined architecture allows us to integrate components, either in house developed, commercial or open source, such as the visualizer in our SPL case.

We proposed a layered PLA for a meshing tool SPL and we showed that a variety of diverse meshing tools are consistent with the proposed structure. By formally specifying the PLA using xADL, we were also able to iterate until we designed an architecture that was simple enough to be easily understood, while general enough to be able to capture the abstractions behind a wide variety of meshing tools. Having an integrated graphical and textual modeling tool such ArchStudio, greatly helped in this process.

The proposed PLA can be used as a road map to build almost any meshing tool. Different dimensions, algorithms, strategies and criteria will determine the concrete implementation of the component types identified as part of the PLA that will be part of each different meshing tool. We plan to build a more complete set of different implementations of the component types in the PLA and a software framework based on the PLA structure as a "meshing tool factory" for designing different tools that may be automatically built by combining the chosen implementation for each component type.

There are currently some astronomical applications being developed based on the proposed PLA, mainly using the proposed layered structure as a guideline.

Acknowledgments

The work of Nancy Hitschfeld-Kahler was partially supported by Fondecyt Project N°1061227. The work of Pedro O. Rossel was partially supported by grant No. UCH 0109 from MECESUP, Chile.

References

1. ArchStudio 3. Architecture-Based Development Environment. Institute for Software Research, University of California, Irvine, 2005. http://www.isr.uci.edu/projects/archstudio/.
2. Len Bass, Paul Clements, and Rick Kazman. *Software Architecture in Practice.* SEI Series in Software Engineering. Addison-Wesley, 2nd edition, 2003.
3. María Cecilia Bastarrica and Nancy Hitschfeld-Kahler. Designing a product family of meshing tools. *Advances in Engineering Software*, 37(1):1–10, January 2006.
4. María Cecilia Bastarrica, Marcelo López, Sergio F. Ochoa, and Pedro O. Rossel. Using the Integrated Notation for Defining a Product Line Architecture. In *Proceedings of the First Conference on the PRInciples of Software Engineering, PRISE'04*, Buenos Aires, Argentina, November 2004.
5. María Cecilia Bastarrica, Sergio F. Ochoa, and Pedro O. Rossel. Integrated Notation for Software Architecture Specifications. In *Proceedings of the XXIV International Conference of the Chilean Computer Science Society, SCCC'04*, pages 26–35, Arica, Chile, November 2004. IEEE Computer Society.
6. Jan Bosch. *Design and Use of Software Architectures. Adopting and Evolving a Product Line Approach.* Addison Wesley, first edition, May 2000.
7. Frank Buschmann, Regine Meunier, Hans Rohnert, and Peter Sommerlad. *Pattern Oriented Software Architecture: A System of Patterns.* John Wiley & Son Ltd., August 1996.
8. Paul Clements, Felix Bachmann, Len Bass, David Garlan, James Ivers, Reed Little, Robert Nord, and Judith Stafford. *Documenting Software Architectures. Views and Beyond.* SEI Series in Software Engineering. Addison Wesley, 2002.
9. Paul Clements and Linda M. Northrop. *Software Product Lines: Practices and Patterns.* Addison Wesley, first edition, August 2001.
10. Eric M. Dashofy, André van der Hoek, and Richard N. Taylor. A Comprehensive Approach for the Development of Modular Software Architecture Description Languages. *ACM Transactions on Software Engineering and Methodology*, 14(2):199–245, 2005.
11. M. de Berg, M. van Kreveld, M. Overmars, and O. Schwarzkopf. *Computational Geometry. Algorithms and Applications.* Springer, second edition, 1998.

12. Rod W. Douglass, Graham F. Carey, David R. White, Glen A. Hansen, Yannis Kallinderis, and Nigel P. Weatherill. Current views on grid generation: summaries of a panel discussion. *Numerical Heat Transfer, Part B: Fundamentals*, 41:211–237, March 2002.

13. Ahmed H. ElSheikh, W. Spencer Smith, and Samir E. Chidiac. Semi-formal design of reliable mesh generation systems. *Advances in Engineering Software*, 35(12):827–841, 2004.

14. Andreas Fabri, Geert-Jan Giezeman, Lutz Kettner, Stefan Schirra, and Sven Schönherr. On the design of CGAL a computational geometry algorithms library. *Software - Practice and Experience*, 30(11):1167–1202, 2000.

15. Martin Fowler. Who Needs an Architect? *IEEE Software*, 20(5):11–13, 2003.

16. Nancy Hitschfeld, Paolo Conti, and Wolfgang Fichtner. Mixed Element Trees: A Generalization of Modified Octrees for the Generation of Meshes for the Simulation of Complex 3D Semiconductor Device Structures. *IEEE Transactions on Computer-Aided Design of Integrated Circuits and Systems*, 12(11):1714–1725, November 1993.

17. Nancy Hitschfeld-Kalher, Carlos Lillo, Ana Cáceres, María Cecilia Bastarrica, and María Cecilia Rivara. Building a 3D Meshing Framework Using Good Software Engineering Practices. In *Proceedings of the 1st International Workshop on Advanced Software Engineering*, Santiago, Chile, August 2006.

18. Rohit Khare, Michael Guntersdorfer, Peyman Oreizy, Nenad Medvidovic, and Richard N. Taylor. xADL: Enabling Architecture-Centric Tool Integration with XML. In *34th Annual Hawaii International Conference on System Sciences (HICSS-34)*, Maui, Hawaii, January 2001. IEEE Computer Society.

19. Carlos Lillo. Analysis, Design and Implementation of an Object-Oriented System that allows to Build, Improve, Refine and Visualize 3D Objects. Master's thesis, Departamento de Ciencias de la Computación, Universidad de Chile, 2006. (in Spanish).

20. Nenad Medvidovic and Richard Taylor. A Classification and Comparison Framework for Software Architecture Description Languages. *IEEE Transactions on Software Engineering*, 26(1), January 2000.

21. Silvio Merazzi, Edgar Gerteisen, and Andrey Mezentsev. A generic CAD-mesh interface. In *Proceedings of the 9th Annual International Meshing Roundtable*, pages 361–370, October 2000.

22. Anton V. Mobley, Joseph R. Tristano, and Christopher M. Hawkings. An Object-Oriented Design for Mesh Generation and Operation Algorithms. In *Proceedings of the 10th Annual International Meshing Roundtable*, Newport Beach, California, U.S.A., October 2001.

23. Malcolm Panthaki, Raikanta Sahu, and Walter Gerstle. An Object-Oriented Virtual Geometry Interface. In *Proceedings of the 6th Annual International Meshing Roundtable*, pages 67–81, Park City, Utah, U.S.A., 1997.

24. Sunghwan Roh, Kyungrae Kim, and Taewoong Jeon. Architecture Modeling Language based on UML 2.0. In *Proceedings of the 11th Asia-Pacific Software Engineering Conference (APSEC 2004)*, pages 663–669, Busan, Korea, November 2004. IEEE Computer Society.

25. Robert Schneiders. Meshing software, 2006. `http://www-users.informatik.-rwth-aachen.de/ roberts/software.html`.

26. H. Si and Klaus Gärtner. Meshing Piecewise Linear Complexes by Constrained Delaunay Tetrahedralizations. In *Proceedings of the 14th International Meshing Roundtable*, September 2005.

27. R. Bruce Simpson. Isolating Geometry in Mesh Programming. In *Proceedings of the 8th International Meshing Roundtable*, pages 45–54, South Lake Tahoe, California, U.S.A., October 1999.

28. Spencer Smith and Chien-Hsien Chen. Commonality Analysis for Mesh Generating Systems. Technical Report CAS-04-10-SS, Department of Computing and Software, McMaster University, October 2004.

29. Anne Taulavuori, Eila Niemelä, and Päivi Kallio. Component documentation—a key issue in software product lines. *Information and Software Technology*, 46(8):535–546, 2004.

30. Timothy J. Tautges. The common geometry module (CGM): A generic, extensible, geometry interface. In *Proceedings of the 9th Annual International Meshing Roundtable*, pages 337–347, New Orleans, U.S.A., October 2000.

31. Rob C. van Ommering. Building product populations with sofware components. In *Proceedings of the 22rd International Conference on Software Engineering, ICSE 2002*, pages 255–265, Orlando, Florida, USA, May 2002. ACM.

32. Rob C. van Ommering, Frank van der Linden, Jeff Kramer, and Jeff Magee. The Koala Component Model for Consumer Electronics Software. *IEEE Computer*, 33(3):78–85, 2000.

33. David M. Weiss and Chi Tau Robert Lai. *Software Product-Line Engineering: A Family Based Software Development Process*. Addison-Wesley, 1999.

A Model for Capturing and Tracing Architectural Designs

M. Luciana Roldán, Silvio Gonnet, Horacio Leone

CIDISI, Universidad Tecnológica Nacional

INGAR, Universidad Tecnológica Nacional, CONICET

Avellaneda 3657, 3000, Santa Fe, Argentina

{lroldan, sgonnet, hleone}@ceride.gov.ar

Abstract. Software architecture constitutes the primary design of a software system. Consequently, architectural design decisions involved in architecture design have a key impact on the system in such aspects as future maintenance costs, resulting quality, and timeliness. However, the applied knowledge employed and the design decisions taken by software architects are not explicitly represented in the design despite their important role; consequently, they remain in the mind of designers and are lost with time. In this work, a model for capturing and tracing the products and architectural design decisions involved in software architecture design processes is proposed. An operational perspective is considered in which design decisions can be modelled by means of design operations. The basic ontology of situation calculus is adopted to formally model the evolution of a software architecture.

1   Introduction

Software Architecture Design Process (SADP) involves several activities such as exploration, evaluation and composition of design alternatives which make it a difficult, complex process [1]. In order to address those activities, the research community has been working intensively in the achievement of modelling languages [2, 3], design methods [4] and computer environments for architect assistance [1, 5]. Those tools are basically focused on assisting designers in generating a software architecture design to satisfy a set of requirements. However, documentation of associated rationale, design decisions, and applied knowledge are often omitted. Such omissions stem from the fact that such information may be intuitive or obvious to the architects involved in the design process, or from the lack of adequate computer-aided environments that allow support design processes. Thus, most

Please use the following format when citing this chapter:

Roldán, M.L., Gonnet, S., Leone, H., 2006, in IFIP International Federation for Information Processing, Volume 219, Advanced Software Engineering: Expanding the Frontiers of Software Technology, eds. Ochoa, S., Roman, G.-C., (Boston: Springer), pp. 16–31.

architectural design knowledge and architectural design decisions taken through SADP remain in the minds of experienced designers, and are lost with time. Consequently, capturing design decisions is of great importance to capitalize previous designs and to provide the foundations for learning and training activities. Precisely, this latter issue has been the goal of other contributions [6, 7] which recognise that the design rationale should be incorporated into the SADP.

Therefore, this work introduces a model for capturing and tracing the SADP and its products. Its goals are to make explicit the states of the SADP and the way in which they were generated. The model is based on a generic Process Version Administration Model (PVAM) [8], which provides mechanisms for capturing and managing versions generated during the course of an engineering design project.

In the next section a conceptual model is presented, introducing the extensions for making PVAM applicable to SADP. After that, the operation capturing system is described, where the products and operations of the SADP are represented. The proposed model is illustrated in Section 4 with a case study about the design of a monitoring system for an industrial process. Finally, conclusions and future research guidelines are discussed.

2   A Conceptual Model for Capturing Architectural Design Processes

The proposed scheme considers the SADP as a sequence of activities operating on the products of the design process, which are called *design objects*. Examples of *design objects* are components and connectors of the architecture being designed, or functional and quality requirements and scenarios to be met. Naturally, these objects evolve as the SADP takes place, giving rise to several versions. In order to maintain these versions, the previously proposed PVAM [8] is considered. The general scheme employed in such approach represents a *design object* at two levels, the *repository* and the *versions level*. Each *model version* is generated from views of a *repository* that keeps all the objects that have been created and modified due to the model evolution during a design project. The elements constituting the *repository* are called *versionable objects*. A *versionable object* represents the artifact that can evolve during a design project, whose history is desirable to be kept during the modelling process. Furthermore, relationships among the different objects are maintained in the *repository*.

At the *versions level*, the evolution of *versionable objects* contained in the *repository* is explicitly represented. A *model version* consists of a set of instances of *object versions* which represent the versions of the objects that compose a given model at a time point. The relationships between a *versionable object* and one of its *object versions* is represented by the *version*(v, o) predicate. Therefore, a given *versionable object* keeps a unique instance in the *repository* and the *versions* it assumes in different *model versions* belong to the *versions level*.

Based on that scheme, the model evolution is posed as a history made up of discrete situations. The situation calculus [9] is adopted for modelling such version generation process. A new model version m_n is generated when an activity a is executed. An activity a is materialised by a sequence of operations ϕ and the new model version m_n is the result of applying such sequence ϕ to the components of a previous model version m_p. In the context given by the design process, it is possible to assimilate each new generated *model version* with a *situation* and each *action* with a *sequence of operations* which is applied on a precedent model version. Therefore, the new model version m_n is achieved by performing the following evaluation: $apply(\phi, m_p) = m_n$.

The primitive operations that were proposed to represent the transformation of *model versions* are *add*, *delete*, and *modify*. By using the *add(v)* operation, an *object version* that did not exist in a previous *model version* can be incorporated into a successor *model version*. Conversely, the *delete(v)* operation eliminates an *object version* that existed in the previous *model version*. Also, if a *design object* has a version v_p, the *modify(v_p, v_s)* operation creates a new *version* v_s of the existing *design object*, where v_s is a successor *version* of v_p. Thus, an *object version* v is *added* after applying the sequence of operations ϕ to *model version* m when the new version v is created by means of an *add* or *modify* operation (Expression 1). On the other hand, the Expression 2 represents the fact that an *object version* v is *deleted* after applying the sequence of operations ϕ to *model version* m when the version v is deleted by the *delete* or *modify* operation.

$$(\forall \phi, v, m)\ add(v) \in \phi \vee (\exists v_p)\ modify(v_p, v) \in \phi \Rightarrow added(v, apply(\phi, m)) \quad (1)$$

$$(\forall \phi, v, m)\ delete(v) \in \phi \vee (\exists v_s)\ modify(v, v_s) \in \phi \Rightarrow deleted(v, apply(\phi, m)) \quad (2)$$

From these definitions, and using the format of successor state axioms proposed by [9], a formal specification of the cases in which an *object version* belongs to a *model version* is presented. In Expression 3, the predicate *belong(v, m)* is true when *object version* v belongs to model version m. Thus, an *object version* v belongs to a *model version* that arises after applying the sequence of operations ϕ to *model version* m, if and only if one of the following conditions is met: (i) v is added when the new *version* is created (*added(v, apply(\phi, m))*); or (ii) v already belonged to the previous *model version* m (*belong(v, m)*) and it is not deleted when ϕ is applied to it (*¬deleted(v, apply(\phi, m))*).

$$(\forall \phi, v, m)\ belong(v, apply(\phi, m)) \Leftrightarrow$$
$$(belong(v, m) \vee added(v, apply(\phi, m))) \wedge (\neg deleted(v, apply(\phi, m))) \quad (3)$$

From this expression, the *object versions* belonging to a *model version* can be determined. Then, it is possible to reconstruct a *model version* m_{i+1} by applying all operation sequences from the initial *model version* m_0.

Once the versions belonging to a *model version* are defined, the relationships existing among *object versions* have to be specified. First, it should be noted that in this proposal, *object versions* belonging to a *model version* are not explicitly associated to other versions belonging to the same model version. These links are represented at the repository level. Consequently, the relationship existing between two object versions must be inferred from the relationship established between the versionable objects that have been versioned by them. This fact is represented in

Expression 4, in which an association a_k is inferred between two object versions v_1 and v_2 belonging to the same model version m ($inferredAssociation(a_k, v_1, v_2, m)$), if and only if there exists an association a_k between the two versionable objects o_1 and o_2 ($association(a_k, o_1, o_2)$), of which v_1 and v_2 are versions, respectively ($version(v_1, o_1)$ and $version(v_2, o_2)$).

$$(\forall\ v_1, v_2, m, a_k)\ inferredAssociation(a_k, v_1, v_2, m) \Leftrightarrow$$
$$(\exists\ o_1, o_2)\ belong(v_1, m) \wedge belong(v_2, m) \wedge version(v_1, o_1) \wedge version(v_2, o_2) \wedge$$
$$association(a_k, o_1, o_2) \qquad (4)$$

The primitive operations *add*, *delete*, and *modify* introduced are not enough to capture and trace a SADP execution. Then, PVAM must be extended in terms of the suitable operations for this design domain, like the ones listed in Table 1. This operations range from the most basic to the most complex ones:

- *Basic*: operations that allow creating and deleting basic design objects (like *components* and *connectors*);
- *Special*: more complex operations that involve object refinement or delegation;
- *Styles/Mechanisms application*: these operations generate a new set of design objects which have a configuration based on an architectural style; or even if they do not modify the model structure, they affect certain design objects properties.

Table 1. Possible Operations for the Software Architecture Design Domain

Basic Operations		
addComponent	addScenario	deleteQualityRequirement
addConnector	addTypeComponent	deleteResponsibility
addFunctionalRequirement	addTypeConnector	deleteRole
addPort	deleteComponent	deleteScenario
addProperty	deleteConnector	deleteTypeComponent
addQualityRequirement	deleteFunctionalRequirement	deleteTypeConnector
addResponsibility	deletePort	
addRole	deleteProperty	
Special Operations		
refineComponent	delegateResponsibility	verifyScenario
refineResponsibility	delegateScenario	
Styles/Mechanisms application		
applyIntermediaryBlackboard	applyRuleEngine	applyPoolOfConnections
applyControlLoop	applyClientServer	

These operations are defined in terms of primitive operations as $add(c)$, and non-primitive ones (see Table 1), as $addPort(c, p)$. The execution of one of these operations implies that a sequence of primitive operations *add*, *delete*, and/or *modify* are applied to a previous model version, which results in a new model version. From this, it is possible to express these operations in terms of *added* and *deleted* predicates introduced in Expressions 1 and 2. For illustration purposes, let us consider the $addComponent(s, c, l_{Resps}, l_{Ports})$ operation. It adds a component c to a system s. Therefore, if it is applied to a model version m, then a version of a component c having a set of *responsibilities* r and *ports* p, will belong to the successor model version ($apply(\phi, m)$), as it is defined in Expression 5.

$$
\begin{aligned}
(\forall\ \phi, s, c, l_{Resps}, l_{Ports}, m)\ addComponent(s, c, l_{Resps}, l_{Ports}) \in \phi \Rightarrow \\
added(c, apply(\phi, m)) \wedge added(rel(s,c), apply(\phi, m)) \wedge \\
((\forall\ r \in l_{Resps})\ added(r, apply(\phi, m)) \wedge added(rel(c,r), apply(\phi, m))) \wedge \\
((\forall\ p \in l_{Ports})\ added(p, apply(\phi, m)) \wedge added(rel(c,p), apply(\phi, m)))
\end{aligned} \tag{5}
$$

Similarly to Expression 5, the definition of new operations allows enlarging the set of operations. This can be done without modifying the successor state axiom (Expression 3).

The precondition for applying the *addComponent* operation is specified in Expression 6, where the $poss(op, m)$ predicate expresses that an operation op is applicable to a given model version m.

$$
\begin{aligned}
(\forall\ s, c, l_{Resps}, l_{Ports}, m)\ poss(addComponent(s, c, l_{Resp}, l_{Ports}), m) \Leftrightarrow \\
belong(s, m) \wedge \neg\ belong(c, m) \wedge \\
(\forall\ r \in l_{Resps})\ \neg\ belong(r, m) \wedge (\forall\ p \in l_{Ports})\ \neg\ belong(p, m)
\end{aligned} \tag{6}
$$

3   The Version Support System for Capturing Architectural Design Processes

3.1   Defining the Operations Model

The class diagram illustrated in Fig. 1 shows the main concepts of PVAM introduced in the previous section. The relationship between a *versionable object* and one of its *object versions* is represented by the *version* relationship. Furthermore, it is assumed that design objects are identified and classified according to the different types (see Section 3.2). The design object type is represented by *ModellingConcept* class (Fig. 1).

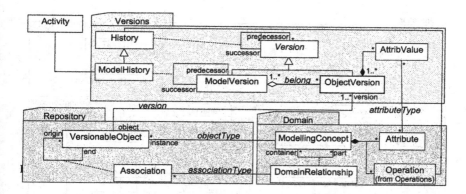

As outlined before, each transformation operation applied to a *model version* incorporates the necessary information to trace a model evolution. This information is represented by *history* relationships between the *object versions* to which the *operation* is applied and the ones arising as the result of its execution (Fig. 1). In order to represent architecture evolution, a model version has zero or more successor model versions (noted by * cardinality at *successor* role of *History* association shown in Fig. 1).

PVAM must be capable of extending in terms of the suitable operations for SADP domain. Subsequently, in this section the operation model is presented, which allows specifying and instantiating specific domain operations.

Operations are associated with a *modelling concept* and are defined as ordered sets of commands (Fig. 2). Those commands can be *primitives* or *operations* that can be used to define other operations. *Primitives* encapsulate the semantics defined by Expressions 1, 2 and 3. The execution of an *operation* generates one or more *results*, which can be a set of *versions*. Furthermore, *history* class is instantiated, linking the *predecessor* with the *successor versions*.

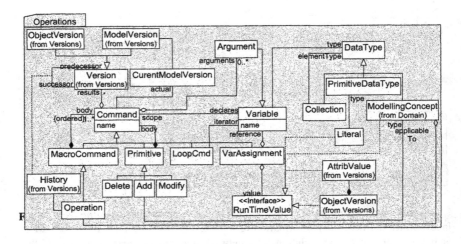

The operation definition is represented using the basic structure of the Abstract Syntax Kernel Metamodel for Expressions defined by the UML 2.0 OCL Specification [10]. To implement operations, the well-known Command design pattern was used [11]. Therefore, a *command* abstract class is introduced into the *Operations* package illustrated in Fig. 2. An *operation* is defined as a *macro command* (*MacroCommand* class), a subclass of *command* that simply executes a sequence of commands. Therefore, when an operation is specified, it is necessary to define both the *arguments* and the *body* of the operation. The commands that constitute its body are some other already defined commands, which are available for use in the specification (primitives, loop, variable assignment, or other operations). Note that the *modelling concept* over which an operation is applied must be explicitly indicated. Furthermore, there are other concrete classes that specialise the *command* class, and that can be part of a *macro command*. One of them is the *LoopCmd*, which represents a loop construct over a collection variable and has a body that is executed for each element in the collection. Another valid command is *VariableAssignment* that represents the assignment of a value to a variable of a given type.

As shown in Fig. 2, every *command* has one or more data typed *arguments*. *Arguments* are considered as a kind of *variable*. A *variable* can be also declared and used in the body of an *operation* and has a given type. The types described by the model are grouped by the abstract class *DataType*. *DataType* subclasses are *PrimitiveDataType*, *CollectionType*, and *ModellingConcept*. *PrimiteDataType* includes *Integer*, *Float*, *String* and *Boolean* types. *Collection* describes a list of elements of a particular given type that are ordered, have no duplicates and are parameterized with an element type. *ModellingConcept* is imported from *Domain Package* and enables specifying arguments that explicit the type of an expected object version to be added during the execution of an *add* primitive.

As regards *VariableAssignment*, it denotes the mapping between a *Variable* and a *RunTimeValue*. This interface is not defined to specify operations. It is included to represent the run time values during the execution of an operation. *RunTimeValue* can be realized by different values like *literal, object version, modelling concept,* or *AttribValue* (value of an attribute of an object version, Fig. 2), depending on the variable type.

3.2   Products of SADP

In order to capture the versions generated during a SADP, the PVAM must be extended according to the particular design objects produced by that process. To this purpose, the *Domain Package* shown in Fig. 1 must be extended with concepts of the SADP domain. The products that constitute the design object types are taken from the Attribute-Driven Design Method (ADD) proposed in [4], and the architectural description language ACME [2]. The class diagram shown in Fig. 3 introduces these concepts and their relationships. This model is implemented by the instantiation of the classes of *Domain package* (Fig. 1). The classes presented in Fig. 3 are going to be instances of *ModellingConcept* and their properties are going to be instances of *Attribute*. Finally, the relationships of Fig. 3 will be instantiated from *DomainRelationship* in *Domain package*.

The ADD method is based on a recursive decomposition process where architectural patterns (or *styles*) are chosen at each stage to fulfil a set of *quality scenarios*. Then, *component* and *connector types* provided by architectural patterns are instantiated and functionality is allocated to them. The input to ADD is a set of requirements (*functional* and *quality requirements*). The *quality requirements* are expressed as a set of system specific *quality scenarios*, and the *functional requirements* are translated into a set of *responsibilities* [4]. Quality scenarios and responsibilities can be delegated to other components when the original component is refined. When the method iteration is finished, the designer verifies scenarios and sets an *assessment*.

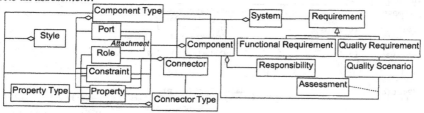

Fig. 3. Domain model for architecture based design

In ADD, the different model versions are represented using various types of views. Only the component view is considered within the scope of this work in order to describe the architecture. Accordingly, ACME [2] has been chosen as the architectural description language. ACME defines a *component* as a computational element and data store of a system. A *component* may have multiple interfaces, each of which is termed *port*. The *connectors* represent interactions among *components* and have interfaces that are defined by a pair of *roles*. The *systems* comprise *components* and *connectors*, establishing *attachments* between *roles* and *ports*. In

Fig. 3, the *attachment* concept is not considered as a *modelling concept* but as a relationship. Moreover, ACME proposes elements to document extra-structural properties of a system's architecture, as *Properties*. Furthermore, it is possible to attach *constraints* to design elements. With the aim of providing a more powerful language, ACME defines *component, connector,* and *property type* building blocks. On the basis of these modelling concepts, it is possible to define *Families* or *Styles*. They are defined by a set of *property, component,* and *connector types* and a set of *constraints*.

3.3   Architectural Operations Specification

As it was outlined in Section 3.1, PVAM must be extended in terms of the suitable operations for the SADP domain, like the ones listed in Table 1.

Fig. 4 presents functional specifications for some of the basic operations defined in Table 1. The other operations are defined in a similar way, but they are not shown due to lack of space. As seen in Fig. 4, the operation *addComponent*(s, c, l_{Resps}, l_{Ports}) is carried out by a series of operations. First, a version of component c is added (*add*(c)). After that, a set of responsibilities (specified by list l_{Resp}) and ports (detailed by list l_{Ports}) are inserted. These operations are carried out by the *addResponsibility*(c, r) and *addPort*(c, p) operations. Finally, a relationship between the new component c and an existing system s is included. This last operation is performed by the *add* primitive operation (*add*(*rel*(s, c))). These operation specifications are implemented as instances of the *Operation* model introduced in Fig. 2.

In the same way as for basic operation, it is possible to define the special operations. Fig. 5 presents some examples. A function with a '?' symbol at the end indicates that it is interactive; thus, the user is asked about how to proceed. The interactive commands can be implemented as a special case of *VarAssignment* command (Fig. 2).

```
addComponent(s,c, lResps,lPorts)       deleteComponent(s, c)
   add(c)                                 lPorts = getPorts(c)
   for each r in lResps                   for each p in lPorts
      addResponsibility(c,r)                 deletePort(c, p)
   end for                                end for
   for each p in lPorts                   delete(rel(s,c))
      addPort(c, p)                       delete(c)
   end for
   add(rel(s, c))

addPort(c, p)                          deletePort(c, p)
   add(p)                                 // port deletion implies deletion
   add(rel(c, p))                         // of connector attached to it
                                          deleteConnector(getConnector(getRol(p)))
                                          delete(rel(c, p))
                                          delete(p)

addResponsibility(c, r)                deleteResponsibility(c, r)
   add(r)                                 delete(rel(c, r))
   add(rel(c, r))                         delete(r)
```

Fig. 4. Specifications of basic operations

The *delegateResponsibility*(c_1, c_2) operation enables delegating a responsibility of component c_1 to component c_2. Thus, if a given responsibility is assigned to a component c_1 in a model version m and a *delegateResponsibility*(c_1, c_2) operation is included in the sequence of operations applied to m, then the resulting model version shows that the responsibilities delegated to c_2 will not be assigned to c_1. In a similar way, the operation *delegateScenario* proceeds.

```
delegateResponsibility(c1, c2)           delegateScenario(c1, c2)
    lResps = getResponsibility(c1)            lScens = getScenario(c1)
    for each r in lResps                      for each s in lScens
        if (delegate?(c2, r))                     if (delegate?(c2, s))
            delete(rel(c1, r))                        delete(rel(c1, s))
            add(rel(c2, r))                           add(rel(c2, s))
        end if                                    end if
    end for                                  end for
refineComponent(c, lComps, lIPorts, lIResps , lConns, lIRoles, lIAtts)
    i = 0
    for each cc in lComps
        lr = lIResps(i) // cc responsibilities listi
        lp = lIPorts(i) // cc ports listi
        addComponent(getSystem(c),cc,lr,lp)
        i++
    end for
    i = 0
    for each cn in lConns
        lr = lIRoles(i) // cn roles listi
        la = lIAtts(i) //  port list which should attach cn roles
        addConnector(getSystem(c), cn, lr, la)
        i++
    end for
    // delegate scenarios and responsibilities to new components
    // (interactive)
    for each cc in lComps
        delegateScenario(c, cc)
        delegateResponsibility(c, cc)
    end for
    // create new connections between internals and external components
    // (interactive)
    lp = getPorts(c)
    for each p in lp
        np = PortMap?()
        r = getRol(p)
        delete(rel(p, r))
        add(rel(np, r))
    end for
    deleteComponent(getSystem(c),c)
```

Fig. 5. Specifications of special operations

The *refineComponent(c, l_{Comps}, l_{IPorts}, l_{IResps}, l_{Conns}, l_{IRoles}, l_{IAtts})* operation, another example of special operation (Fig. 5), decomposes a component c into one or more components given by the list l_{Comps}. The ports and responsibilities of the new components are given by the lists l_{IPorts} and l_{IResps}, respectively. Furthermore, a set of connectors among the new components is added. These connectors are specified by l_{Conns} whose roles are given by the list l_{IRoles} and the attachments by the list l_{IAtts}.

The operations that apply an architecture style [12], or an architectural pattern [13], refine a preexistent component with a new set of components and connectors that are instantiated from an architectural style/pattern. They interact with the designer asking for the responsibilities and scenarios delegation, as well as connectors mapping between external components and refined components. An example of *applyStyle* operation is defined in Fig. 6. In this case, the *applyControlLoop* operation is specified. This style proceeds from the process control paradigm and defines the architecture to activate various monitoring policies when different events coming from sensors are produced [14]. The monitoring policies may in turn produce other events or actions in response to predefined situations. Note that this operation can be considered as a specialization of *refineComponent* operation. The knowledge on how to proceed in the refinement of component *c* is given by the control loop style. Therefore, a series of *addComponent* operations is performed. The *addComponent*(*s*, {*Diagnosis*, *TDiagnosis*}, [P_1,P_6]) operation indicates that a component and two ports must be created. The component is called *Diagnosis*, whose modelling concept is *TDiagnosis*, an instance of *ComponentType* (see Fig. 3), and the ports are denominated P_1 and P_6.

```
applyControlLoop(c)
    s = getSystem(c)
    addComponent(s,{Diagnosis, TDiagnosis}, [P1,P6])
    addComponent(s,{PolicyManager, TPolicyManager}, [P2,P3])
    addComponent(s,{Reactor, TReactor}, [P4, P5])
    addConnector(s,{CDgnPMgr,TCDgnPMgr},[R1,R2],[P1,P2])
    addConnector(s,{CPMgrRct,TCPMgrRct},[R3,R4],[P3,P4])
    delegateScenario(c,Diagnosis)
    delegateScenario(c,PolicyManager)
    delegateScenario(c,Reactor)
    delegateResponsibility(c,Diagnosis)
    delegateResponsibility(c,PolicyManager)
    delegateResponsibility(c,Reactor)
    // Set mappings between previous connector and new components
    lp = getPorts(c)
    for each p in lp
        np = PortMap?(p) // Ask the user the port to map
        r = getRol(p)
        delete(rel(p, r))
        add(rel(np, r))
    end for
    deleteComponent(s, c)
```

Fig. 6. Specification of applyControlLoop operation

4   Case Study: Monitoring System for an Industrial Process

The following case study describes the design of a monitoring system for an industrial process (see Fig. 7). It is based on classical case studies presented in other contributions [1, 4]. Monitoring activities are focused on the two core distillation columns: an extractive distillation column and a solvent stripping one, working together in a highly integrated manner. The system should monitor control loops and temperature sensors, by continued acquisition of real-time process data, tracking set-point values, alarm conditions and outputs of valves, and comparing them with normal pattern behaviour. The system should also monitor process state, using real-time process data previously processed in combination with expert knowledge in order to maintain process stability and performance. Further functionalities are control flowrate sensors and validate material balances. In order to meet all these functional requirements, the system should be connected to input and output devices. Input devices allow the system to get the real time data from the process equipment and output devices are used by the system to inform the plant operator about process anomalies, like: solvent inventory buildup, sensor fault, abnormal process pattern, etc. The main functions considered in designing the monitoring system include: administration of users (process operator, plant supervisor, etc.) and permissions, configuration of input/output devices, priority-based event management, process diagnosis, specification of warning and process protective actions.

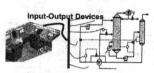

Fig. 7. Monitoring system for an industrial process

For reasons of space, only a sequence of operations of the model evolution is analyzed. Let us consider an intermediate *model version i* (see Fig. 8) where the main components are: *Control&Diagnosis* (with responsibilities in priority based event management, protective actions execution, warning launch, input/output devices configuration); *UserInterface* (with responsibilities related to user interaction issues: set parameters values, show information, rule administration); *SensorActuatorLayer* (with responsibilities like sending out commands to actuators, receiving information from sensors); and *Configuration*. From this model version, the designer chooses to refine the *Control&Diagnosis* component by applying the *applyControlLoop* operation. This operation creates three new *components*: *Diagnosis*, *PolicyManager*, and *Reactor*. The *applyControlLoop* operation (see Fig. 6) asks the necessary information for delegating responsibilities, and for reconnecting previous connections to the new configuration.

Fig. 8 shows a partial view of the *Version* and *Repository* levels from which model version views can be inferred. This figure is focused on the version of *Control&Diagnosis* evolution to a set of versions of components and connectors due to *applyControlLoop* operation. A *view* of a *model version* is obtained from the knowledge in the *Version* and *Repository* levels. The object versions belonging to a *model version* are inferred by the $belong(v, m)$ predicate (Expression 3). Fig. 8 shows some object versions that belong to *model version i* ($Control\&Diagnosis_{v,1}$, $P1C\&D_{v,1}$, $P2C\&D_{v,1}$, $P3C\&D_{v,1}$). Given an object version ($Control\&Diagnosis_{v,1}$), it is possible to know its versionable object ($Control\&Diagnosis_o$), which is linked with its design object type (modelling concept *component*, defined in *Domain*). All this information makes possible to reconstruct the elements of a model version view, as it is the *Control&Diagnosis* component which is obtained from object version $Control\&Diagnosis_{v,1}$ and versionable object $Control\&Diagnosis_o$. On the other hand, the expression 5 enables to retrieve the relationships among the object versions that belong to a given model version. $Control\&Diagnosis_o$ has three ports named $P1C\&D_o$, $P2C\&D_o$, and $P3C\&D_o$ which have their respective object versions $P1C\&D_{v,1}$, $P2C\&D_{v,1}$, and $P3C\&D_{v,1}$. Therefore, component $Control\&Diagnosis_{v,1}$ has ports $P1C\&D_{v,1}$, $P2C\&D_{v,1}$, and $P3C\&D_{v,1}$.

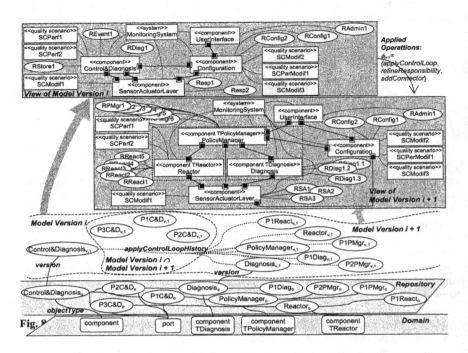

Fig. 9

The *applyControlLoop* operation is applied on *Control&Diagnosis* component (*Control&Diagnosis$_{v,1}$* object version). This operation is traced by an instance of the *history* link (Fig. 1) which associates the previous object version (*Control&Diagnosis$_{v,1}$*) with the successor object versions (*Reactor$_{v,1}$*, *Diagnosis$_{v,1}$*, *PolicyManager$_{v,1}$*, *P1React$_{v,1}$*, *P1Diag$_{v,1}$*, *P1PMgr$_{v,1}$*, *P2PMgr$_{v,1}$* in Fig. 8). *P1C&D$_{v,1}$*, *P2C&D$_{v,1}$*, and *P3C&D$_{v,1}$* object versions belong to both *model version i* and *model version i+1* because they were delegated from the original component (*Control&Diagnosis*) to the newer ones by *applyControlLoop* operation.

Additionally, other operations were applied on model version *i* to obtain model version *i+1* that are not illustrated in Fig. 8 at version and repository levels. One of them arises due to the need of associating *PolicyManager* and *Configuration* components, so a new *connection* and their *roles* objects are added, applying *addConnector* operation. Using again operation *addConnector*, a new connection between *PolicyManager* and *SensorActuatorLayer* is added. It enables *PolicyManager* to receive information from, and send information to, *SensorActuator* (see Fig. 8, *View of model version i+1*).

It is important to note that the proposed extension of PVAM enables applied operations on SADP's products (Fig. 3) to be captured. For example, responsibilities are refined using *refineResponsibility* operation. The *RDiag1* responsibility (Fig. 8, view of model version *i*) was refined on the following responsibilities: i) listening notifications of situations coming from *SensorActuator* (*RDiag1.1*); ii) getting devices information (*RDiag1.2*); iii) probing device (*RDiag1.3*) (Fig. 8, *view of model version i + 1*).

4.1 Retrieving the History of Architectural Design Processes

The model introduced allows tracing and recovering the history of the architectural design activities carried out by the designer during SADP. It is possible to ask about the history of model versions in terms of operation sequences that have generated a given model version, and also consult on the history of a particular object version, which allows to know how the evolution took place through the different versions. Fig. 9 shows an example of a history query to perform on the hypothetical monitoring system designed in current section. An actor would whish to know the sequence of operations that originated model version $i+1$ from the precedent model version i. The applied operations were *applyControlLoop*, *refineResponsibility* and *addConnector*, which can be seen in Fig. 8 of the case study. The resulting information allows knowing who carried out the operations, at what time and date, their arguments, the new elements incorporated to the design, the set of elements eliminated and what kind of modelling concepts they were. As shown in Fig. 9, additional information can be obtained, like the suboperations implied at the execution of the current one. Knowing which were the operations that gave rise to model version $i+1$ is useful for understanding the rationale associated with such a step because the architect knows the semantic of the operation and the intent.

5   Conclusions

The model proposed in this paper, an extension of PVAM, captures the operations that generate each design product during the SADP. Furthermore, it also offers an explicit mechanism to manage the different model versions generated during the SADP. Thus, it allows the tracing of the SADP and its resulting products, setting the grounds for learning and future reuse of the design process. This is a fundamental step towards the development of computational tools to support the SADP and to guide designers in the different activities of a design project. A related work [6] proposes a set of requirements which such tools should satisfy in order to adequately support the evolution of software architectures. The approach presented in this work meets a wide spectrum of those requirements: (i) *First class architectural concepts*, represented by the extensible domain model proposed; (ii) *First class architectural design decisions*, enabling specification of adequate operations for software architecture design representing design decisions made by the architect; (iii) *Under-specification and incompleteness*, allowed by the model evolution through discrete situations (model versions) increasing the level of abstraction; (iv) *Explicit architectural changes*, allowing capturing, managing and tracing of products of SADP, using explicit history links between different versions, which means that the operations applied through the design process are saved and, therefore, it is possible to reconstruct the history from an initial model version; (v) *Support for modification, subtraction, and addition type changes*, implemented by the primitive operations add, delete and modify. Those operations are also used in the definition of higher level operations representing more complex design operations like refining or styles application.

Model Version: Model Version i+1
Precedent Model Version: Model Version i
Applied Operations:

Operation: applyControlLoop
Model Version: Model Version i   **Actor:** Architect1
Arguments:

Argument Name	Value	Data Type
Source Version	Control&Diagnosis	Component

Results:

Object Version	Modelling Concept	Date Time
PolicyManager$_{v,1}$	Component TPolicyManager	01-06-2006 10:56
Reactor $_{v,1}$	Component TPolicyManager	01-06-2006 10:56
......	......	......
RPMgr1 $_{v,1}$	Responsibility	01-06-2006 10:56

Deleted versions:

Object Version	Modelling Concept	Date Time
Control&Diagnosis $_{v,1}$	Component	01-06-2006 10:56
....	.....	....
Rel_C&D_Diag $_{v,1}$	Relation	01-06-2006 10:56

SubOperations:

(+) delegateResponsibility
(+) delegateResponsibility
...

Operation: refineResponsibility
Model Version: Model Version i   **Actor:** Architect1
(+)

Operation: addConnector
Model Version: Model Version i   **Actor:** Architect1
(+)

Fig. 9. Partial view of the sequence of operations applied to model version i

Situation calculus, the formal background of the framework, allows us to represent the activities carried out during a SADP, and therefore, it enables the designer to get a better understanding of the information on how the various design objects (systems, components, connectors, functional requirements, quality requirements, quality scenarios, assessment, etc.) have been obtained. Thus, the history of operations performed on versions of design objects can be kept. Besides, this conceptual framework also provides the foundations for the proposal of formal means for detecting potential conflicts.

The framework could incorporate extensions to the Domain package, integrated to the version administration model, defining other characteristics not included by ADD or ACME. Furthermore, it uses an operational perspective where design decisions can be modelled by means of design operations. This approach is employed in other contributions [1, 4]. The structure of the conceptual framework allows the easy definition of specific design operations, like *applyControlLoop*, by instantiating the *Operation* model (Fig. 2). This extension is possible without modifying the successor state axiom (Expression 3).

References

1. A. Díaz Pace, *A Planning-Based approach for the exploration of Quality-Driven design alternatives in Software Architectures*, Tesis Doctoral (UNICEN, 2004).
2. D. Garlan, R. T. Monroe, D. Wile, Acme: Architectural Description of Component-Based Systems. *Foundations of Component-Based Systems*, edited by G.T. Leavens and M. Sitaraman (Cambridge University Press, 2000), pp. 47-68.
3. N. Medvidovic, D. Rosenblum, D. Redmiles, J. Robbins, Modeling Software Architectures in the Unified Modeling Language, *ACM Transaction on Software Engineering and Methodology*, 11(1), 2-57 (2002).
4. L. Bass, P. Clements, R. Kazman, *Software Architecture in Practice: Second Edition* (Addison-Wesley, 2003).
5. F. Bachmann, L. Bass, M. Klein, Preliminary Design of ArchE: A Software Architecture Design Assistant, Carnegie Mellon University, Technical Report CMU/SEI-2003-TR-021, 2003.
6. A. Jansen, J. Bosch, Evaluation of Tool Support for Architectural Evolution, in: Proceedings of the 19th IEEE International Conference on Automated Software Engineering (2004), pp. 375-378.
7. A. Tang, J. Han, Architecture Rationalization: A Methodology for Architecture Verifiability, Traceability and Completeness, in: 12th IEEE International Conference and Workshops on the Engineering of Computer-Based Systems (2005), pp. 135-144.
8. S. Gonnet, *Un modelo integrado para la captura y administración del proceso de diseño*, Tesis Doctoral (UNL, 2003).
9. R. Reiter, *Knowledge in Action: Logical Foundation for Describing and Implementing Dynamical Systems* (The MIT Press, 2001).
10. Object Management Group, OCL 2.0 Specification (2005), 2005-06-06.
11. E. Gamma, R. Helm, R. Johnson, K. Vlissides, *Design Patterns. Elements of Reusable Object-Oriented Software* (Addison-Wesley, 1995).
12. M. Shaw, D. Garlan, *Software Architecture, Perspectives on an Emerging Discipline* (Prentice-Hall, 1996).
13. F. Buschmann, R. Meunier, H. Rohnert, P. Sommerlad, M. Stal, *Pattern-Oriented Software Architecture. A System of Patterns* (John Wiley & Sons, 1996).
14. M. Shaw, Beyond Objects: A Software Design Paradigm Based on Process Control, Carnegie Mellon University, Technical Report CMU-CS-94-154, 1994.

Acknowledgments
The authors wish to acknowledge the financial support received from CONICET, Universidad Tecnológica Nacional and Agencia Nacional de Promoción Científica y Tecnológica (PICT 12628).

Multidimensional Catalogs for Systematic Exploration of Component-Based Design Spaces

Claudia López and Hernán Astudillo

Universidad Técnica Federico Santa María, Departamento de Informática
Avenida España 1680, Valparaíso, Chile
clopez @inf.utfsm.cl, hernan @inf.utfsm.cl

Abstract. Most component-based approaches to elaborate software require complete and consistent descriptions of components, but in practical settings components information is incomplete, imprecise and changing, and requirements may be likewise. More realistically deployable are approaches that combine exploration of candidate architectures with their evaluation vis-a-vis requirements, and deal with the fuzzyness of available component information. This article presents an approach to systematic generation, evaluation and re-generation of component assemblies, using potentially incomplete, imprecise, unreliable and changing descriptions of requirements and components. The key ideas are representation of NFRs using architectural policies, systematic reification of policies into mechanisms and components that implement them, multi-dimensional characterizations of these three levels, and catalogs of them. The Azimut framework embodies these ideas and enables traceability of architecture by supporting architecture-level reasoning, and allows architects to engage into systematic exploration of design spaces. A detailed illustrative example illustrates the approach.

1 Introduction

Component-based software development proposes building systems by using pre-existing components, to reduce development time, costs and risks and to improve product quality; achieving these goals requires an adequate selection of components to reuse. Current methods of component evaluation and selection are not geared to support human specialists in the systematic exploration of design spaces because they require complete and consistent descriptions of components behavior, connections and prerequisites. In the real-world software architects have at hand incomplete, imprecise and changing component information, and requirements may be likewise.

This article presents a process and tool to support software architects in the exploration of design spaces by enabling generation, evaluation and regeneration of component assemblies. The Azimut framework deals with the fuzzyness of component information using incomplete "characterizations" of available components and allowing the regeneration of assemblies when better information about components is obtained.

Please use the following format when citing this chapter:

López, C., Astudillo, H., 2006, in IFIP International Federation for Information Processing, Volume 219, Advanced Software Engineering: Expanding the Frontiers of Software Technology, eds. Ochoa, S., Roman, G.-C., (Boston: Springer), pp. 32–46.

The reminder of this article is structured as follows: Section 2 provides a brief overview of related work; Section 3 introduces the process of generation, evaluation and regeneration of component assemblies, and the concepts of *architectural policies and mechanisms*; Section 4 describes the structure of the *multi-dimensional catalogs*, and illustrates the approach with an example; Section 5 describes the automation of derivation process and its implementation in a prototype; Sections 6 and 7 discuss ongoing work and conclusions.

2 Systematic Processes for Selecting Components

Component-Based Software Development (CBD) [19] suggests reusing existing components to build new systems, attending to benefits like shorter development times, lower costs and higher product quality. Thus, a key ingredient of CBD is component selection.

Some proposed techniques for component evaluation and selection [2–9] identify reuse candidates using criteria such as functionality, non-functional requirements (NFRs) or architectural restrictions that each component and/or the whole system must satisfy. Some of these proposals [5–8] give semi-automated support to the selection process using multi-criteria decision support techniques, such as AHP (Analytic Hierarchy Process) [12] or WSM(Weighted Scoring Method).

Most approaches [2–9] require complete and consistent descriptions of component behavior, connections and prerequisites, but in practice architects have at hand incomplete, imprecise and changing component information. Accepting this fuzzyness and dealing with it is a key step to supporting the actual COTS selection process.

Also, several proposals [2–7] only explore the space of available components without recourse to alternative designs at intermediate abstraction levels. These approaches force architects to deal with a big gap between the component and requirement spaces, and to describe exhaustively the relationships between them. Working with intermediate abstraction levels enables dealing with smaller gaps and searching smaller spaces. CRE [8] and CARE/SA [9] use the NFR Framework [10] to derive more specific requirements or design solutions when considering quality attributes or NFRs; unfortunately, the NFR Framework does not explicitly distinguish requirements more detailed than the design solutions that satisfy them, and the derivation process among them depends on the architect's knowledge of possible refinements, without recourse to a systematic and possible automated derivation support.

3 Exploration, Generation and Evaluation of Component Assemblies

Our larger research goal is supporting iterative exploration of design spaces by human architects, and keeping traceability of the resulting architectural decisions. The Azimut project focuses on enabling architects to generate component assemblies [15] for some given requirements; evaluate and compare these assemblies regarding their requirements satisfaction and some higher-order criteria (e.g. economic, risk); and regenerate assemblies when new or better information is available.

The conceptual vocabulary underlying our approach is description of selection decisions using the concepts of architectural policies and architectural mechanisms.

3.1 Architectural Policies and Mechanisms

Architects may reason about the overall solution properties using architectural policies, and later refine them (perhaps from existing policy catalogs) into artifacts and concepts that serve as inputs to software designers and developers, such as component models, detailed code design, standards, protocols, or even code itself. Thus, architects define policies for specific architectural concerns and identify alternative mechanisms to implement such policies. For example, an availability concern may be addressed by fault-tolerance policies (such as master-slave replication or active replication) and a security concern may be addressed by access control policies (such as identification-, authorization- or authentication-based) [16].

Each *reification* yields ever more concrete artifacts; thus, architectural decisions drive a process of successive reifications of NFRs that end with implementations of mechanisms that do satisfy these NFRs.

To characterize such reifications, we use a vocabulary taken from the distributed systems community [14], duly adapted to the software architecture context:

Architectural Policies: The first reification from NFRs to architectural concepts. Architectural policies can be characterized through specific concern dimensions that allow describing NFRs with more details.

Architectural Mechanisms: The constructs that satisfy architectural policies. Different mechanisms can satisfy the same architectural policy, and the differences between mechanisms is the way in which they provide certain dimensions.

As a brief example (taken from [24]), consider inter-communication among applications. One architectural concern is the communication type, which might have the dimensions of sessions, topology, sender, and integrity v/s timeliness [18]; to this we add synchrony. Then, the requirement *send a private report to subscribers by Internet* might be mapped in some project (in architectural terms) as requiring communication 'asynchronous, with sessions, with 1:M topology, with a push initiator mechanism, and priorizing integrity over timeliness'. Based on these architectural requirements, an architect (or automated tool!) can search a catalog for any existing mechanisms or combination thereof that provides this specified policy; lacking additional restrictions and using well-known software, a good first fit as mechanism is SMTP (the standard e-mail protocol), and thus any available component that provides it.

3.2 Systematic Generation of Component Assemblies

To illustrate how these concepts relate and are used in practice consider the following example (see Figure 1. The derivation process starts from quality attribute that may be associated to specific *architectural concerns* (e.g. access control for security requirements, replication for availability). Architectural concerns can be characterized through *dimensions*, which are discriminating factors among policies (e.g. authentication type [16] in access control, update pro pagation type [17] for replication). Each dimension can be satisfied by some *architectural policies* (e.g. authentication based-on-something-that-the-user-knows, operations-based update propagation). Each policy may be satisfied by several *architectural mechanisms* (e.g. SMTP-AUTH for authentication based-on-something-that-the-user-knows, active replication for replication with state-based update propagation). Finally, mechanisms may be provided by one or more available *components*, which in turn may implement several mechanisms (e.g.SendMail v8.1 and later for SMTP-AUTH; LifeKeeper for active SMTP server replication en Linux).

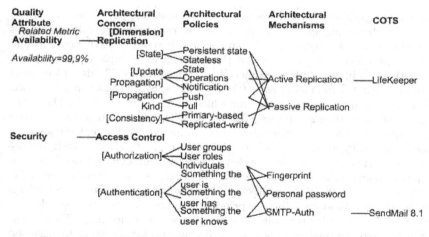

Fig. 1. Example of Systematic Generation of Component Assemblies

The selected components are organized in alternative assemblies that aim to satisfy all the systemic properties at once. Assemblies are later subject to evaluation choose among them using some system-wide criteria (e.g. cost, or smallest number of suppliers). This process is described in Figure 2.

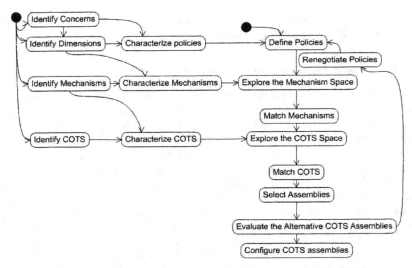

Fig. 2. Generation and Evaluation of Component Assemblies

3.3 Systematic Exploration of Design Spaces

Architects repeatedly perform derivations from systemic properties to possible solutions, identifying and evaluating those that each architectural mechanisms provides, as well as each selected component. These alternative solutions and reifications are the design space that the architect must explore, and which is currently done in an intuitive manner. As shown in Figure ??, after identifying potential architectural mechanisms ('Match Mechanisms') comes an exploration of the components space to determine which ones implement them. The result is a set of alternative components ('Match COTS') from which the alternate component assemblies are generated to be evaluated. Notice that the solution space is generally quite large, highly changing and in constant growth, mainly due to the dynamic components market. In an open market of independent component developers, the set of possible combinations is not known to any of the involved parties [19]. The architect's knowledge of architectural mechanisms and available components (held a priori or acquired in the ongoing selection process) is the basis for reasoning that justifies selection decisions. Thus, keeping in catalogs information about which mechanisms satisfy which policies and which components implement which mechanisms allows sharing this valuable knowledge; and identifying derivation rules allows supporting, and perhaps even semi-automating, the exploration process performed by architects.

Alternative assemblies can be evaluated to select the one that best fits the specified requirements, matches the platform restrictions, and meets the non-technical selection criteria, such as minimal cost, minimal number of suppliers, and maximal suppliers' reliability.

When new information becomes available, or when requirements change, regeneration of component assemblies is called for. New assemblies may include other mechanisms and/or new components, or in fact drop some and consolidate others. To support these generation, evaluation and regeneration processes, and the consequent design space exploration, we deploy multi-dimensional catalogs to characterize policies, mechanisms and components, and systematic derivation rules among these levels, as shown in Figure 3 and explained in Section 4.

4 Multi-dimensional Catalogs

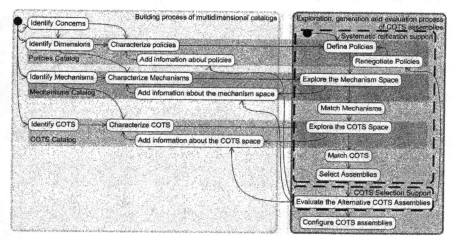

Fig. 3. Multidimensional Catalogs for Exploration, Generation and Evaluation of Component Assemblies

Catalogs store architects' knowledge about architectural policies, mechanisms and components, as well as the derivation rules among them. Thus, they are the key to reusing information about previous selection processes; improving knowledge quality about design spaces and components insofar as better descriptions are stored; and supporting architects in the exploration of these design spaces.

Figure 3 describes the two roles that catalogs fulfill: as repositories of information necessary to generate, evaluate and regenerate component assemblies; and as actively maintained descriptions of the components available in a given milieu. The parallelism and mutual feedback of these two processes allow to use catalog information and derivation rules for selection decisions, and to add information to the catalog when some ongoing selection process gathers additional data.

This section will illustrate the deployment and use of catalogs with a running example. Consider propagation of stock prices information, and the requirement *'the system shall send a report to each customer according to his stocks portfolio; this service must have 99.9% availability and provide access security.'*

4.1 Policy Catalogs

The *policy catalogs* gathers platform-independent architectural policies and stores dimensions for each concern and policies that have different values for each dimension. The catalog incorporates knowledge for each architectural concern, and the dimensions themselves are collected from authoritative sources of the relevant discipline (e.g. Tanenbaum [17] for replication, Britton [18] for middleware communication, and Firesmith [16] for security). Figure 4 shows a partial content of the policies catalog.

Choosing among the policies shown in Figure 4, we notice that the system requires Asynchronous Communication Type, with 1:M topology, with Push initiator, and communication must privilege Integrity over Timeliness. Security is focused on Access Control, and the usual policies are Individual Authorization and Authentication based on something the user knows [20]. Availability is represented by several architectural concerns, such as Replication, Recovery and Failure Monitoring; here, we'll use only Replication. To meet the availability requirement, we define replication policies with Persistent State and Replicated Write Consistency.

Independently of the suggested use of catalogs as stepping stones in larger derivation chains, it should be noticed that even a stand-alone catalog of architectural policies (however incomplete) would be useful to help in representing (and thus negotiating and validating) quality attributes, as long as the relevant concerns, dimensions and policies are present.

4.2 Mechanism Catalogs

The *mechanism catalog* records known architectural mechanisms, which are implementation-independent design-level constructs that satisfy architectural policies. This catalog indicates which mechanisms satisfy which policies, and characterizes each mechanism with the values of each concern dimension that it can satisfy. A given mechanism may implement several policies for a same concern, or policies across several concerns; similarly, a given policy may be implemented by several mechanisms. Figure 5 shows partial content of the mechanisms catalog.

In real-world deployment situations, the catalog preparators might not know or not be certain whether a given mechanism supports a certain policy. To account for this uncertainty, the mechanisms catalog allows five degrees of certainty regarding support for a given policy: 'supports'(1), 'probably supports'(0,6),'probably does not support'(0,3), 'does not support'(0), and

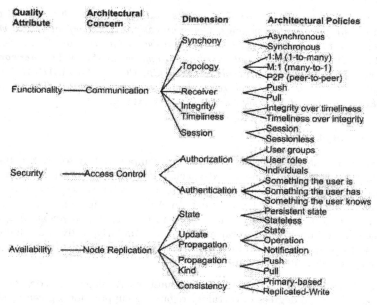

Fig. 4. Partial Content of Policies Catalog

'unknown'(empty) (since absence of knowledge differs from knowledge of absence). Incidentally, current work is using fuzzy optimization techniques on these uncertainty-rich descriptions to evaluate and regenerate component assemblies.

Architectural Mechanisms	Asynchronous	Synchronous	1:M (many-to-one)	M:1 (one-to-one)	P2P (peer-to-peer)	Push	Pull	Integrity over timeliness	Timeliness over integrity	Session	Sessionless	User Groups	User Roles	Individuals	Something that user is	Something the user has	Something the user knows	Persistent state	Stateless	State	Operation	Notification	Push	Pull	Primary-Based	Replicated-Write
SMTP	1	0	1	0	0	1	0	1	0	1	0															
IM	0	1	0	0	1	1	0	1	1	0																
NNTP	1	0	1	0	0	0.8	0	1	0	1	0															
RSS	1	0	1	0	0	0	1	1	0	1	0															
POP3	0	1	0	1	0	0	1	1	0	1	0															
IMAP	0	1	0	1	0	0	1	1	0	1	0															
SIP	0	1	0	0	1	0	1	0	1	0	1															
SMTP-Auth												0	0	1	0	0	1									
POP-Auth												0	0	1	0	0	1									
MAP-Auth												0	0	1	0	0	1									
Active Replication																		1	0	0	1	0	1	0	0	1
Passive Replication																		1	0	1	0	0	1	0	1	0
Voting																		0	1							
Personal Password												0	0	1	0	0	1									
ID Card												0	0	1	0	1	0									
Fingerprint												0	0	1	1	0	0									

Fig. 5. Partial Content of Mechanisms Catalog

The catalog shown in Figure 5 sugggests that the architect has several options to satisfy the specified policies: Communication Type may me reified with the NNTP *protocol (used to post subscription-based "news") or* SMTP *(used to send e-mail). The Access Control policies might be satisfied with a* **personal password** *mechanism. The protocols SMTP-Auth, POP-Auth, IMAP-Auth and Personal Password do satisfy the requirements of Access Control. The replication policies can be satisfied with* **active replication**.

4.3 Components Catalog

The *component catalog* describes the space of components. A software component [19] is multiple-use, non-context-specific, composable with other components, encapsulated (i.e., non-investigable through its interfaces) and a unit of independent deployment and versioning. In Azimut, components are characterized according to the architectural mechanism(s) that implement. A given component may implement several mechanisms; similarly, a given mechanism may be implemented by several components. Besides mechanism support, the components catalog has four dimensions:

- **Uncertainty** Just Similarly to the mechanisms catalogs, the components catalog allows five degrees of certainty regarding support for a given mechanism: 'supports', 'probably supports', 'probably does not support', 'does not support', and 'unknown'.
- **Available platforms** Platform(s) under which the component can be deployed (e.g. Windows, Linux, Solaris).
- **Market issues** Component selection requires using non-technical criteria to distinguish among otherwise equivalent alternate components and assemblies. The catalog includes some key characteristics: Supplier; Market Share [11]; Supplied Reliability [6] (valued from 1 to 5, with higher values for higher reliability); Initial Cost [11]; Integration Cost [11]; and Support Cost.
- **Description credibility** An important criterion is the credibility degree [5] of the component description, which quantifies confidence regarding descriptions. We follow Philips and Polen [5] in assigning credibility values for descriptions: (1) user- or supplier-provided, or seen in third-party literature; (2) seen but not studied; (3) witnessed in personalized demos; and (4) verified hands-on "in-house".

Figure 6 shows partial content of a components catalog relevant to the running example.

Several mechanism configurations are possible, and in fact some components do implement each desired mechanism. Components that implement mechanisms that satisfy all required quality attributes are **LifeKeeper** *and* **SendMail** *(v8.1 and later; notice that earlier versions might also be recorded in the catalog); or* **SurgeMail (Cluster)**. *Choosing among them means having an additional goal function: if it is minimizing number of components (to reduce complexity), the optimal solution is* **SurgeMail (Cluster)**, *but if it is minimizing costs,*

Architectural Mechanisms	SMTP	IM	NNTP	RSS	POP3	IMAP	SIP	SMTP-Auth	POP-Auth	IMAP-Auth	Active Replication	Passive Replication	Voting	Personal Password	ID Card	Fingerprint	VB + patch
SendMail	1	0	0	0	0	0	0	1	0	0							
CourierMailServer	1	0	0	0	1	1	0	0,6	0,6	0,6				0	0		
SurgeMail	1	0	0	0	1	1	0	0,6	0,6	0,6				0	0		
DNews	0	0	1	0	0	0	0	0	0	0							
LeafNoad	0	0	1	0	0	0	0	0	0	0							
CyrusIMAPServer	0	0	0	0	1	1	0	0	0,6	0,6				0	0		
LifeKeeper	0	0	0	0	0	0	0	0	0	0	0,6	0,6					
SurgeMail(Cluster)	1	0	0	0	0	0	0	0,6	0,6	0,6	0,6	0,6		0	0		

Fig. 6. Partial Contents of Components Catalog

the other option is better. Other alternatives are looking for additional information (and enrich the catalogs); considering ad-hoc implementation of passive replication; or outsourcing the replication service and defining in the SLA an availability target of 99.9%. At this point, active exploration of design spaces by the architect should ensue.

Another difference between catalogs is the global and authoritative nature of the policies and mechanisms catalog versus the local nature of the component catalog in each organization. In fact, there might be sub-catalogue suppliers for a global component information repository.

4.4 Recording Feedback into Catalogs

A better evaluation could inject some new information to the selection process as well: new descriptions (characterizations) of components and mechanisms to increase the knowledge of solutions spaces, or new policies to better describe some requirements; or it might suggest renegotiation of requirements if impossible to find any assemblies that satisfy all given requirements (see Figure 3).

Thus, an additional advantage of these catalog-based process is that exploration of mechanisms and components feeds back into the catalog construction process (see Figure 3).

5 Automation of Derivation Process

Based on the several platform abstraction levels, we can identify derivation rules among them (the relationships 'provides' among mechanisms and policies, and 'implements' among components and mechanisms), as well as combination restrictions. Automating these derivation rules allows proposing components and assemblies dynamically to the architect. Currently, we are at work in two alternative approaches to achieving automation: one rule-based (herein shown), and one based on combinatorial optimization algorithms [?]. Both approaches try to avoid the complexity of assigning weights to the influence of each solution element (mechanism, component) on each goal, unlike AHP (the multi-criteria decision technique used by several CBD methods [5–8]).

Combinatorial optimization techniques have allowed us to explore some very interesting problems, like treatment of fuzzy data (such as 'probably supports'), information variability at the level of both requirements and components, treatment of conflict among mechanisms or components as restrictions, and incompatible combinations.

Azimuy possibly uses incomplete, imprecise, unreliable and changing descriptions of architectural policies, mechanisms and components. As mentioned above, these characteristics allow using the catalogs even during early definition stages, to help with requirements definition and validation.

Later on, assemblies that are proposed in the absence of full knowledge (i.e. catalogs with several 'unknown' entries) may turn out to be sub-optimal regarding number of components or some other criterion, but new information will not necessarily invalidate it (unless it generates a conflict).

Fuzzy information is a normal situation in architecture development, since incomplete and imprecise information is what most architects actually have at hand. Accepting this fuzzyness and dealing with it is a key step to supporting actual architects elaborating actual software systems.

5.1 Rule-based Prototype

We have developed a prototype to validate the feasibility of this approach. Rules [27] describe the "characterizations" of policies, mechanisms, and components, and relationships among them and the other attributes. Using these rules, the system generates component assemblies that satisfy the required policies. The prototype deals with fuzzyness by showing first solutions based on 'supports' and 'implements', and later the fuzzy attributes, but currently it optimizes for simples non-technical attributes (e.g. minimum number of components, or total cost). Examples of these rules are shown in Table 1.

Figure 7 shows the output given by the prototype when you search assemblies satisfying the policies of our example.

6 Ongoing and Future Work

Work in progress includes expanding the kinds of recorded information in catalogs; identifying further derivation rules; implementing algorithms to treat fuzzy information [25]; and managing conflicts among mechanisms or components.

Also, some computationally hard problems are being studied jointly with combinatorial optimization researchers to analyze trade-offs among several selection criteria; what-if analysis to quantify the impact of requirements changes; and reverse questioning, i.e. determining satisfiable requirements given a set of components.

Table 1. Rules

satisfies(smtp,[asynchronous,synchrony,communication_type]).
satisfies(smtp,[1:m,topology,communication_type]).
satisfies(smtp,[push,receiver,communication_type]).
satisfies(smtp,[integrity_over_timeliness,integrity/timeliness,communication_type]).
satisfies(active_replication,[persistent_state,state,node_replication]).
satisfies(active_replication,[replicatedwrite,consistency,node_replication]).
satisfies(smtp_auth,[individuals,authorization,access_control]).
satisfies(smtp_auth,[something_the_user_knows,authentication,access_control]).
satisfies(rss,[asynchronous,synchrony,communication_type]).
satisfies(rss,[1:m,topology,communicatin_type]).
satisfies(rss,[pull,receiver,communication_type]).
probablySatisfies(nntp,[push,receiver,communication_type]).
satisfies(nntp,[integrity_over_timeliness,integrity/timeliness,communication_type]).
....

implements(sendMail,smtp). implements(sendMail_v8_1,smtp).
implements(sendMail_v8_1,smtp_auth). implements(surgeMailCluster,smtp).
implements(dNews,nntp). implements(leafNoad,nntp).
probablyImplements(lifeKeeper,active_replication).
probablyImplements(lifekeeper,passive_replication).
probablyImplements(surgeMailCluster,smtp_auth).
probablyImplements(surgeMailCluster,active_replication).
....

notRelatedCots(lifeKeeper,dNews). notRelatedCots(lifeKeeper,leafNoad).
notRelatedCots(lifeKeeper,surgeMailCluster).

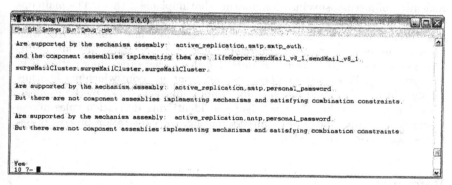

Fig. 7. Prototype: Output for the example

6.1 Application: MDA

Model-Driven Architecture (MDA) [21] aims to derive/generate software systems through systematic transformations from high-level models. Some projects, such as CoSMIC [22] and UniFrame [23], implement MDA to generate component-based systems, but use formal component specification languages to describe the available components, and from these descriptions (consistent and precise) they automate the component selection and integration process.

However, in most systems without strong constraints like hard real-time, the cost of using formal specifications is difficult to justify; thus, we aim to integrate incomplete, imprecise, unreliable and changing descriptions into MDA techniques. Current systematic techniques to select components are hard to integrate with MDA due to the lack of explicit mappings among PIM-level concepts of analysis and design, and PSM-level constructs such as components.

We have deployed the described approach and techniques in the Azimut framework [24], which extends MDA to automate architectural decisions from NFRs through components. The prototype is described in [26].

7 Conclusions

The described process to generate, evaluate and regenerate component assemblies, combined with the multi-dimensional catalogs that support it, allows architects to engage in iterative exploration of design spaces. A key goal of this exploration is finding the "best" combination of components that not only satisfy the given requirements, but also fit some non-technical second-order criteria (such as minimal cost or maximal supplier reliability), but accepting the fuzzy nature of available component information.

The underlying concepts are representation of quality attributes using architectural policies, their systematic reification into architectural mechanisms, and reification of mechanisms into components that implement them. The main operational feature of the approach are *catalogs* for three abstraction levels (policies, mechanisms and components); these abstractions are "characterize" with possibly *incomplete, imprecise, unreliable and changing* data, and are *multidimensional* in including technical data but also higher-order information (e.g. cost, supplier). Thus, keeping in catalogs information about which mechanisms satisfy which policies and which components implement which mechanisms allows sharing this valuable knowledge; and identifying derivation rules allows supporting, and perhaps even semi-automating, the exploration process of design spaces performed by architects.

References

1. Sihem Ben Sassi, Lamia Labed Jilani, Henda Hajjami Ben Ghezala: "COTS Characterization Model in a COTS-Based Development Environment." APSEC 2003, p. 352.
2. Ncube, C., Maiden, N. "PORE: Procurement-Oriented Requirements Engineering Method for the CBSE Development Paradigm." International Workshop on CBSE, May 1999.

3. Alves, C., Finkelstein, A.: "Challenges in COTS-Making: a Goal-Driven Requirements Engineering Perspective." Proc. 14th Intl. Conf. on Software Engineering and Knowledge Engineering (SEKE'02), Italy (July 2002).

4. Ochs, M.: "A COTS Acquisition Process: Definition and Application Experience." 11th ESCOM Conference, Shaker, Maastricht, 2000.

5. Philips, B., Polen, S.: "Add Decision Analysis to Your COTS Selection Process." The Journal of Defense Software Engineering, Software Technology Support Center Crosstalk, April 2002.

6. Kontio, J.: "A case study in applying a systematic method for COTS selection." Proceedings ICSE 1996, p. 201-209.

7. Kunda, D., Brooks, L.: "Applying Social-Technical Approach to COTS Selection." Proceedings 4th UKAIS Conference, Abril 1999.

8. Alves, C., Castro, J.: "CRE: A Systematic Method for COTS Components Selection." 15th Brazilian Symposium on Software Engineering (SBES), Rio de Janeiro, Brazil (Oct 2001).

9. Chung, L., Cooper, K.: "COTS-Aware Requirements Engineering and Software Architecting." Proceedings IWSSA 2004

10. Chung, L.,Nixon, B., Yu, E., Mylopoulos, J.: *Non-Functional Requirements in Software Engineering*. Kluwer Academic Publisher, 2000.

11. Chin Yeoh, H., Miller, J.: "COTS Acquisition Process: Incorporating Business Factors in COTS Vendor Evaluation Taxonomy." METRICS 2004, pp. 84-95.

12. Saaty, T.: "The Analytic Hierarchy Process". New York: McGraw-Hill, 1990.

13. Albin, S.: *The Art of Software Architecture: Design Methods and Techniques.* Wiley, Mar 2003.

14. Policy and Mechanism Definitions. http://wiki.cs.uiuc.edu/MFA/Policy+and+Mechanism

15. Vitharana, P.,Fatemah "Mariam" Zahedi, Jain, H.: "Design, retrieval, and assembly in component-based software development." Commun. ACM (46)11, Nov 2003, p.97-102.

16. Firesmith, D.: "Specifying Reusable Security Requirements." Journal of Object Technology, 3(1), pp.61-75 (Jan-Feb 2004). http://www.jot.fm/issues/issue_2004_01/column6

17. Tannenbaum, A., van Steen, M.: *Distributed Systems Principles and Paradigms.* Prentice Hall (2002).

18. Britton, C., Bye, P.: *IT Architectures and Middleware: Strategies for Building Large, Integrated Systems (2nd Ed).* Addison-Wesley Professional (2004).

19. Szyperski, C.: *Component Software* (2nd Edition). Addison-Wesley Professional(2002).

20. Authentication Mechanisms. http://sarwiki.informatik.hu-berlin.de/Authentication_Mechanisms

21. *MDA Guide Version 1.0.1.* Object Management Group (June 2003). http://www.omg.org/cgi-bin/doc?omg/03-06-01

22. Gokhale, A., Balasubramanian, K., and Lu, T. "CoSMIC: Addressing Crosscutting Deployment and Configuration Concerns of Distributed Real-Time and Embedded Systems." OOPSLA 2004, ACM Press, p. 218-219.

23. Cao, F., Bryant, B., Raje, R., Auguston, M., Olson, A., Burt. C: "A Component Assembly Approach Based on Aspect-Oriented Generative Domain Modeling." ENTCS 2005, pp.119-136.

24. López, C., Astudillo, H.: "Explicit Architectural Policies to Satisfy NFRs using COTS." Workshop NfC 2005 in MoDELS'2005, Oct 2005. In: *Satellite Events at the MoDELS 2005 Conference*, Bruel, Jean-Michel (Ed.), LNCS 3844, pp. 227 - 236, Springer (Jan 2006).
25. Astudillo, H., Pereira, J., López, C.: "Evaluating Alternative COTS Assemblies from Unreliable Component Information." Technical Report DI-2006/05, Departamento de Informática, Universidad Técnica Federico Santa María, Valparaíso, Chile (2006).
26. Montenegro, A., Astudillo, H.: "Generation of hybrid code+COTS systems." Technical Report DI-2006/06, Departamento de Informática, Universidad Técnica Federico Santa María, Valparaíso, Chile (2006).
27. SWI Prolog Documentation. http://www.swi-prolog.org/

Practical Verification Strategy for Refinement Conditions in UML Models

Claudia Pons [1,2] and Diego Garcia [3,1]

[1]LIFIA – Facultad de Informática, Universidad Nacional de La Plata
[2]CONICET (Consejo Nacional de Investigaciones Científicas y Técnicas)
[3]UTN (Universidad Tecnológica Nacional)
La Plata, Buenos Aires, Argentina
{cpons,dgarcia}@sol.info.unlp.edu.ar

Abstract. This paper presents an automatic and simple method for creating refinement condition for UML models. Conditions are fully written in OCL, making it unnecessary the application of mathematical languages which are in general hardly accepted to software engineers. Besides, considering that the state space where OCL conditions are evaluated might be too large (or even infinite), the strategy of micromodels is applied in order to reduce the search space. The overall contribution is to propitiate the performing of verification activities during the model-driven development process.

1. Introduction

The stepwise refinement technique facilitates the understanding of complex systems by dealing with the major issues before getting involved in the details. The system under development is first described by a specification at a very high level of abstraction. A series of iterative refinements may then be performed with the aim of producing a specification, consistent with the initial one, in which the behavior is fully specified and all appropriate design decisions have been made.

Stepwise software development can be fully exploited only if the language used to create the specifications is equipped with formal refinement machinery, making it possible to prove that a given specification is a refinement of another specification, or even to calculate possible refinements from a given specification. Robust refinement machinery is present in most formal specification languages such as Object-Z [21], B [11], and the refinement calculus [2], and even in some restricted forms of programming languages [4]. However, the widely-used standard specification language UML [15] lacks for a well-defined notion of refinement.

To alleviate this problem most research on the formalization of UML refinements adhere to the approach of mapping the graphical notation into a formal domain where properties are defined and analyzed. For example the works presented in [1], [5], [7], [10], [12], [13] and [22] among others, belong to this group. They are appropriate to discover and correct inconsistencies and ambiguities of the graphical language, and in most cases they allow us to verify and calculate refinements of (a restricted form of)

Please use the following format when citing this chapter:

Pons, C., García, D., 2006, in IFIP International Federation for Information Processing, Volume 219, Advanced Software Engineering: Expanding the Frontiers of Software Technology, eds. Ochoa, S., Roman, G.-C., (Boston: Springer), pp. 47–61.

UML models. However, such approaches are non-constructive (i.e., they provide no feedback in terms of UML), they require expertise in reading and analyzing formal specifications and generally, properties that should be proved in the formal setting are too complex or even undecidedly.

In [18] and [19] we explored an alternative approach, as a complement to the former; well founded refinement structures in the Object-Z formal language were used to discover refinement structures in the UML, which are (intuitively) equivalent to their corresponding Object-Z inspiration sources. A similar proposal was presented in [3], where Boiten and Bujorianu explore refinement indirectly through unification; the formalization is used to discover and describe intuitive properties on the UML refinements. On the other hand, Liu, Jifeng, Li and Chen in [14] use a formal specification language to formalize and combine UML models; then, they define a set of refinement laws of UML models to capture the essential nature, principles and patterns of object-oriented design, which are consistent with the refinement definition.

In this article we work further on those proposals by enriching such refinement patterns with refinement conditions written in OCL (Object Constraint Language) [16]. The advantage of this approach is that refinement conditions get completely defined in terms of OCL, making it unnecessary the application of languages which are usually hardly accepted by software engineers. OCL is a more familiar language and it has a simpler syntax than Object-Z and other formal languages. Additionally, OCL is part of the UML 2.0 standard and it will probably form part of most modeling tools in the near future.

Furthermore, after defining refinement conditions, the next step is to evaluate such conditions. Ordinary OCL evaluators are unable to determine whether a refinement condition written in OCL holds in a UML model because OCL formulas are evaluated on a particular instance of the model, while refinement conditions need to be validated in all possible instantiations. Therefore, in order to make the evaluation of refinement conditions possible, we extract from the UML model a relatively small number of small instantiations, and check that they satisfy the refinement conditions to be proved. This strategy, called *micromodels of software* was proposed by Daniel Jackson in [9] for evaluating formulas written in Alloy. Later on, Martin Gogolla and colleges in [8] developed a useful adaptation of such technique to verify UML and OCL models. Here we adapt such micromodels strategy to verify refinement conditions.

The structure of this document is as follows: sections 2 serves as a brief introduction to the issue of refinement specification in Object-Z and UML 2.0; section 3 describes the method for creating OCL refinement condition for UML refinement patterns; section 4 explains how the micromodels strategy is applied to verify refinements; finally, the paper closes with a presentation of conclusions and future directions.

2. Refinements Specification in Object-Z and UML

In Object-Z [21], a class is represented as a named box with zero or more generic parameters. The class schema may include local type or constant definitions, at most one state schema and an initial state schema together with zero or more operation schemas. These operations define the behavior of the class by specifying any input and output together with a description of how the state variables change. Operations are defined in terms of two copies of the state: one undecorated copy which represents the before-sate and a primed copy representing the after-state.

For example, figure 1 illustrates the specification of a simple class called Flight, having a state (consisting of two variables) and only one operation.

```
Flight
  ↾ (freeSeats, reserve)
  freeSeats: ℕ
  canceled: B

  INIT
  freeSeats=300
  canceled=false

  reserve
  Δ(freeSeats)
  freeSeats>0 ∧ ¬canceled
  freeSeats'=freeSeats-1
```

Figure 1: simple Object-Z schema.

Object-Z is equipped with a schema calculus, that is to say a set of operators provided to manipulate Object-Z schemas. The schema calculus makes it possible to create Objects-Z specifications describing properties of other Object-Z specifications. To deal with refinements we need to apply at least the following operators:

- Operator STATE denotes the set of all possible states (i.e., snapshots or bindings) of the system under consideration. For example, $Flight.STATE = \{\langle freeSeats=x, canceled=t\rangle \mid 0 \le x \le 300 \wedge t \in \{true, false\}\}$

- Operator INIT denotes the initial states of a given schema. For example, $Flight.INIT = \{\langle freeSeats=300, canceled=false\rangle \mid \rangle\}$

- Operator pre returns the precondition of an operation schema; that is to say the set of all states where the operation can be applied. For example, pre reserve = $\{\langle freeSeats = x, canceled=false \rangle \mid 0<x \le 300\}$

- The conjunction of two schemas S and T ($S \wedge T$) results in a schema which includes both S and T (and nothing else).

- Schema implication ($S \Rightarrow T$) denotes the usual logical implication.

In [6] refinement is formally addressed in the context of Object-Z specifications as follows: an Object-Z class C is a refinement (through downward simulation) of the class A if there is a *retrieve relation* R on $A.STATE \wedge C.STATE$ so that every visible abstract operation A.op is recasted into a visible concrete operation C.op thus the following holds:

(Initialization) $\forall$C.STATE $\bullet$ C.INIT $\Rightarrow$ ($\exists$A.STATE $\bullet$ A.INIT $\wedge$ R)
(Applicability) $\forall$A.STATE $\bullet$ $\forall$C.STATE$\bullet$ R $\Rightarrow$ (pre A.op $\Rightarrow$ pre C.op)
(Correctness) $\forall$A.STATE$\bullet$$\forall$C.STATE$\bullet$$\forall$C.STATE'$\bullet$

$\quad$ R $\wedge$ pre A.op $\wedge$ C.op $\Rightarrow$ $\exists$A.STATE'$\bullet$ R' $\wedge$ A.op

This definition allows preconditions to be weakened and non-determinism to be reduced. In particular, applicability requires a concrete operation to be defined wherever the abstract operation was defined, however it also allows the concrete operation to be defined in states for which the precondition of the abstract operation was false. That is, the precondition of the operation can be weakened. Correctness requires that a concrete operation be consistent with the abstract one whenever it is applied in a state where the abstract operation is defined. However, the outcome of the concrete operation only has to be consistent with the abstract, but not identical. Thus if the abstract operation allowed a number of options, the concrete operation is free to use any subset of these choices. In other words, non-determinism can be solved.

On the other hand, the standard modeling language UML [15] provides an artifact named *Abstraction* (a kind of Dependency) with the stereotype <<refine>> to explicitly specify the refinement relationship between UML named model elements. In the UML metamodel an Abstraction is a directed relation from a *client* (or clients) to a *supplier* (or suppliers) stating that the client (the refinement) depends on the supplier (the abstraction). The Abstraction artifact has a meta-attribute called *mapping* designated to record the abstraction/implementation mappings (i.e., the counterpart to the Object-Z *retrieve relation*), which is an explicit documentation of how the properties of an abstract element are mapped to its refined versions, and on the opposite direction, how concrete elements can be simplified to fit an abstract definition. The mapping contains an expression stated in a given language that could be either formal or not. The definition of refinement in the UML standard [15] is formulated using natural language and it remains open to numerous contradictory interpretations.

3. Verification strategy for UML refinement patterns

UML refinement patterns [18] [19] document recurring refinement structures in UML models. In this section we describe one of those patterns, the *state refinement pattern*; then we present an algorithm that can be applied on UML models that contain such a pattern in order to automatically create an OCL refinement condition to verify its applicability and correctness. Similar processes were defined to create refinement condition for other patterns in the catalog, but they are not described here due to space limitations.

3.1. The state refinement pattern

A State Refinement takes place when the data structures which were used to represent the objects in the abstract specification are replaced by more concrete or suitable structures; operations are accordingly redefined to preserve the behavior defined in the abstract specification.

An instance of the pattern's structure:

Let M1 be the UML model in figure 2, which is compliant with the structure of the state refinement pattern [19]. M1 contains information about a flight booking system where each flight is abstractly described by the quantity of free seats in its cabin; then a refinement is produced by recording the total capacity of the flight together with the quantity of reserved seats. In both specifications, a Boolean attribute is used to represent the state of the flight (open or canceled). The available operations are reserve to make a reservation of one seat and cancel to cancel the entire flight. A refinement relationship connects the abstract to the concrete specification. The OCL language [16] [20] has been used to specify initial values, operation's pre and post conditions and the mapping attached to the refinement relationship.

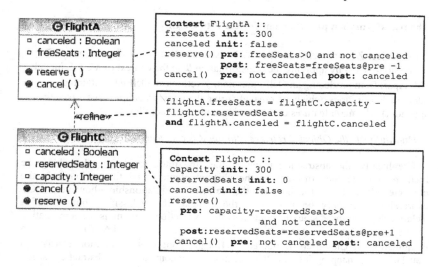

Figure 2: an instance of the state refinement pattern

An instance of the pattern's refinement condition:

Object-Z refinement conditions - F1 - for UML classes FlightA and FlightC via some retrieve relation R are automatically generated from the generic refinement condition established by the pattern [19], based on the definition of downward simulation in Object-Z described in [6]. Figure 3 shows the formula F1.

Initialization
  $\forall$FlightC.STATE •FlightC.*INIT* $\Rightarrow$($\exists$ FlightA.STATE •FlightA.*INIT* $\wedge$ R)

Applicability (of operation reserve)
  $\forall$FlightA.STATE•$\forall$FlightC.STATE •R $\Rightarrow$ (pre FlightA.reserve $\Rightarrow$ pre FlightC.reserve)

Correctness (of operation reserve)
$\forall$FlightA.STATE •$\forall$FlightC.STATE • $\forall$FlightC.STATE'•
  R$\wedge$pre FlightA.reserve $\wedge$ FlightC.reserve $\Rightarrow$ $\exists$FlightA.STATE' •R' $\wedge$ FlightA.reserve

---

Figure 3: an instance of the refinement condition for the state refinement pattern

The transformation process from Object-Z to OCL:

Then, Object-Z refinement condition - F1 - is automatically transformed into OCL expression – F1' - by applying the transformation T in the context of a UML model M1. Apart from producing an OclExpression, T returns an OclFile containing additional definitions, which are created during the transformation process (see the appendix). The main features of the transformation are as follows,

Highlight #1: the Object-Z retrieve relation R is replaced by its OCL counterpart.

Graphically, the abstraction mapping (i.e., the retrieve relation) describing the relation between the attributes in the abstract element and the attributes in the concrete element is attached to the refinement relationship; however, OCL expressions can only be written in the context of a Classifier, but not of a Relationship. On the Z side, the context of the abstraction mapping is the combination of the abstract and the concrete states (i.e., A.STATE $\wedge$ C.STATE); however, a combination of Classifiers is not an OCL legal context. Our solution consists in translating the mapping into an OCL formula in the context of the abstract classifier, in the following way:

```
Context flightA:FlightA def :
mapping(flightC : FlightC):Boolean =
flightA.freeSeats= flightC.capacity -
flightC.reservedSeats and
flightA.canceled= flightC.canceled
```

As a convention, class names in lower case are used to denote instances. It is worth mentioning that the mapping definition could alternatively have been translated into a formula in the context of the concrete classifier.

Highlight #2: Object-Z expression INIT is expressed in terms of an OCL boolean operation isInit().

A query operation isInit() is automatically built from the specification of the attribute's initial values included in the UML class diagram. It returns *true* if all of the instance's attributes satisfy the initialization conditions. For example:

```
context FlightA def: isInit(): Boolean =
self.freeSeats = 300 and self.canceled = false

context FlightC def: isInit(): Boolean =
self.capacity=300 and self.canceled=false and
self.reservedSeats=0
```

Highlight #3: expressions containing the Object-Z operator "pre" are translated into the corresponding OCL pre conditions from the UML model.

For example, the Object-Z expression "**pre** FlightA.reserve" is translated into "flightA.freeSeats>0 **and not** flightA.canceled"

While, the expression "**pre** FlightC.reserve" is translated into "flightC.capacity-flightC.reservedSeats>0 **and** **not** flightC.canceled"

Highlight #4: Object-Z expressions containing operation's invocations are translated to OCL post conditions from the UML model.

In Object-Z, elements belonging to the pre-state are denoted by undecorated identifiers, while elements in the post-state are denoted by identifiers with a decoration (i.e. a stroke). In OCL the naming convention goes exactly in the opposite direction, that is to say, undecorated names refer to elements in the post-state. Then, in order to be consistent with the rest of the specification, a decoration (i.e., "_post") is added to each undecorated identifier in the post condition and the original decoration (i.e., @pre) is removed from the rest of the identifiers. For example the following definition:

```
Context flightA:FlightA::reserve()
 post: flightA.freeSeats= flightA.freeSeats@pre -1
```

is renamed in the following way:

```
Context flightA:FlightA::reserve()
 post: flightA_post.freeSeats= flightA.freeSeats -1
```

Highlight #5: *logic connectors and quantifiers are translated to OCL operators.*

The Z expression $\forall$S.*STATE*•exp is translated to S.allInstances() -> forAll (s | **T**(expr)). The Z expression $\exists$S.STATE•exp is translated to S.allInstances()-> exists(s| **T**(expr)).

Notice that the name of the class, in lower case, is used to name the iterate variable. Finally, the symbol $\Rightarrow$ is translated to ***implies*** and the symbol $\wedge$ is translated to ***and***.

The appendix contains the formal definition of transformations **T** from Object-Z refinement conditions to OCL expressions. On top of that formalization the transformation process was fully automated. Table 1 shows the formula F1' that is the result of applying the transformation **T** on both the UML model M1 (figure 2) and the Object-Z refinement conditions F1 (figure 3).

Table 1: OCL refinement conditions for an instance of the state refinement pattern.

OCL refinement condition
Initialization FlightC.allInstances()->***forAll***(flightC| flightC.isInit() ***implies*** (FlightA.allInstances()-> ***exists***(flightA| flightA.isInit()*and* flightA.mapping(flightC))))
Applicability FlightA.allInstances-> ***forAll***(flightA| FlightC.allInstances-> ***forAll***(flightC| flightA.mapping(flightC) ***implies*** (flightA.freeSeats>0 *and* *not* flightA.canceled ***implies*** flightC.capacity- flightC.reservedSeats>0 ***and not*** flightC.canceled)))
Correctness FlightA.allInstances()-> ***forAll***(flightA| FlightC.allInstances() -> ***forAll***(flightC| FlightC.allInstances()-> ***forAll***(flightC_post| flightA.mapping(flightC) ***and*** (flightA.freeSeats>0 *and* *not* flightA.canceled) ***and*** (flightC_post.reservedSeats = flightC.reservedSeats+1) ***implies*** FlightA.allInstances()-> ***exists***(flightA_post| flightA_post.mapping(flightC_post) ***and*** flightA_post.freeSeats= flightA.freeSeats -1))))

4. Micromodels for evaluating refinement conditions

Generally, UML models specify an infinite number of instances; even little models such as the one described in figure 2 (i.e., there is an infinite number of instances of the type FlightA and an infinite number of instances of the type FlightC); thus to decide whether a certain property holds or not in the model results generally unfeasible.

In order to make the evaluation of refinement conditions viable, the technique of micromodels (or micro-worlds) of software is applied by defining a finite bound on the size of instances and then checking whether all instances of that size satisfy the property under consideration (i.e., the refinement condition):

- If we get a positive answer, we are somewhat confident that the property holds in all instantiations. In this case, the answer is not conclusive, because there could be a larger instantiation which fails the property, but nevertheless a positive answer gives us some confidence.

- If we get a negative answer, then we have found an instantiation which violates the property. In that case, we have a conclusive answer, which is that the property does not hold in the model.

Jackson's small scope hypothesis [9] states that negative answers tend to occur in small worlds already, boosting the confidence we may have in a positive answer.

For example, we will consider micro-worlds of the UML model in figure 2 containing only three instances of Integer and one instance of Boolean. Then we will check whether all micro-worlds of that size satisfy the refinement condition, that is to say:

Applicability Condition for operation reserve():

```
Set{ <0,f>,<1,f>,<2,f> }-> forAll (flightA|
Set{<0,0,f>,<0,1,f>,<0,2,f>,<1,0,f>,<1,1,f>,<1,2,f>,<2,0,f>,
    <2,1,f>,<2,2,f>} ->forAll(flightC|
    flightA.mapping(flightC) implies
    (flightA.freeSeats>0 and not flightA.canceled
    implies flightC.capacity-flightC.reservedSeats>0 and
            not flightC.canceled )))
```

This expression can be easily evaluated by an ordinary OCL evaluator, returning a positive answer, which gives us some confidence that the property holds.

Lets explore a case where the refinement conditions are not satisfied; lets consider for example that preconditions were strengthened in class FlightC,

```
Context flightC:FlightC :: reserve()
pre: flightC.capacity- flightC.reservedSeats>2
     and not flightC.canceled
```

Then, the property to be checked is as follows,

```
Set{ <0,f>,<1,f>,<2,f> }-> forAll (flightA|
Set{<0,0,f>,<0,1,f>,<0,2,f>,<1,0,f>,<1,1,f>,<1,2,f>,<2,0,f>,
    <2,1,f>,<2,2,f>} ->forAll(flightC|
```

```
flightA.mapping(flightC) implies
(flightA.freeSeats>0 and not flightA.canceled
 implies flightC.capacity-flightC.reservedSeats>2 and
         not flightC.canceled )))
```

which evaluates false in any micro-world such that flightA=<2,f> and flightC=<2,0,f> because of the fact that:

```
flightA.mapping(flightC)                              holds,
(flightA.freeSeats>0 and not flightA.canceled) holds,
(flightC.capacity - flightC.reservedSeats > 2) does not hold.
```

Thus, the presence of such micro-worlds gives us the conclusive answer that the refinement property does not hold in the UML model.

6. Conclusion

Abstraction is a cognitive means by which software engineers deal with complexity. The idea promoted by most software development methodologies is to use models at different levels of abstraction; a series of transformations are performed starting from an abstract platform-independent model with the aim of making the model more specific at each step. Each transformation step should be amenable to formal verification in order to guarantee the correctness of the final product.

However, verification activities require the application of formal modeling languages with a complex syntax and semantics and need to use complex formal analysis tools; therefore they are rarely used in practice.

To facilitate the verification task we developed an automatic method for creating refinement conditions for UML models, written in the friendly and well-accepted OCL language. The inclusion of verification in ordinary software engineering activities will be propitiated by avoiding the application of unfamiliar languages and tools.

To complement such method, we adapted a strategy for reducing the search scope in order to make the evaluation of refinement conditions feasible. Since the satisfiable formulas that occur in practice tend to have small models, a small scope usually suffices and the analysis is reliable.

7. References

[1] Astesiano E., Reggio G. An Algebraic Proposal for Handling UML Consistency", Workshop on Consistency Problems in UML-based Software Development. UML Conference (2003).

[2] Back, R. & von Wright, J. *Refinement calculus: a systematic introduction,* Graduate texts in computer science, Springer Verlag. (1998)

[3] Boiten E.A. and Bujorianu M.C. Exploring UML refinement through unification. Proceedings of the UML'03 workshop on Critical Systems Development with UML, J. Jurjens, B. Rumpe, et al., editors -TUM-I0323, Technische Universitat Munchen. (2003).

[4] Cavalcanti A. and Naumann D. Simulation and Class Refinement for Java. In proceedings of ECOOP 2000 Workshop on Formal Techniques for Java Programs. (2000).

[5] Davies J. and Crichton C. Concurrency and Refinement in the Unified Modeling Language. Electronic Notes in Theoretical Computer Science 70,3, Elsevier, 2002.

[6] Derrick, J. and Boiten,E. Refinement in Z and Object-Z. Foundation and Advanced Applications. FACIT, Springer. (2001)

[7] Engels G., Küster J., Heckel R. and Groenewegen L. A Methodology for Specifying and Analyzing Consistency of Object Oriented Behavioral Models. Procs. of the IEEE Int. Conference on Foundation of Software Engineering. Vienna. (2001).

[8] Gogolla , Martin, Bohling, Jo"rn and Richters, Mark. Validation of UML and OCL Models by Automatic Snapshot Generation. In G. Booch, P.Stevens, and J. Whittle, editors, Proc. 6th Int. Conf. Unified Modeling Language (UML'2003). Springer, Berlin, LNCS 2863, (2003).

[9] Jackson, Daniel, Shlyakhter, I. and Sridharan. A micromodularity Mechanism. In proceedings of the ACM Sigsoft Conference on the Foundation of Software Engineering FSE'01. (2001).

[10] Kim, S. and Carrington, D., Formalizing the UML Class Diagrams using Object-Z, proceedings UML'99 Conference, Lecture Notes in Computer Sciencie 1723 (1999).

[11] Lano,K. The B Language and Method. FACIT. Springer, (1996).

[12] Lano,K., Biccaregui,J., Formalizing the UML in Structured Temporal Theories, 2nd. ECOOP Workshop on Precise Behavioral Semantics, TUM-I9813, Technische U. Munchen (1998).

[13] Ledang, Hung and Souquieres, Jeanine. Integration of UML and B Specification Techniques: Systematic Transformation from OCL Expressions into B. Procs. of IEEE Asia-Pacific Software Engineering Conference 2002. December 4-6, (2002).

[14] Liu, Z., Jifeng H., Li, X. Chen Y. Consistency and Refinement of UML Models. 3er. Workshop on Consistency Problems in UML-based Software Development III, event of the UML Conference, (2004).

[15] UML 2.0. The Unified Modeling Language Superstructure version 2.0 – OMG Final Adopted Specification.. http://www.omg.org. August 2003

[16] OCL 2.0. OMG Final Adopted Specification. October 2003.

[17] Pons C., Giandini R., Pérez G., et al. Precise Assistant for the Modeling Process in an Environment with Refinement Orientation. In "UML Modeling Languages and Applications: Satellite Activities". Lecture Notes in Computer Science 3297. Springer, (2004).

[18] Pons Claudia. Heuristics on the Definition of UML Refinement Patterns. 32nd International Conference on Current Trends in Theory and Practice of Computer Science. SOFSEM (SOFtware SEMinar). January 21 - 27, 2006 . Merin, Czech Republic. Published in the Springer LNCS (Lecture Notes in Computer Science) by Springer-Verlag. (2006)

[19] Pons Claudia. On the definition of UML refinement patterns. Workshop MoDeVa at ACM/IEEE 8th Int. Conference on Model Driven Engineering Languages and Systems (MoDELS) Jamaica. October 2005.

[20] Richters, Mark and Gogolla, Martin. OCL-Syntax, Semantics and Tools. in Advances in Object Modelling with the OCL. Lecture Notes in Computer Science number 2263. Springer. (2001).

[21] Smith, Graeme. The Object-Z Specification Language. Advances in Formal Methods. Kluwer Academic Publishers. ISBN 0-7923-8684-1. (2000)

[22] Van Der Straeten, R., Mens,T., Simmonds, J. and Jonckers,V. Using description logic to maintain consistency between UML-models. In Proc. 6th International Conference on the Unified Modeling Language. Lecture Notes in Computer Science number 2863. Springer. (2003).

APPENDIX: transformation from Object-Z to OCL refinement conditions

Grammar for Z refinement expressions:

This section describes the grammar for Z refinement expressions, which is a subset of Object-Z grammar presented in [21].

The grammar description uses the EBNF syntax, where terminal symbols are displayed in bold face. Optional constructs are enclosed by slanted square brackets [].

```
Predicate::=        ∃ SchemaText • Predicate
                    | ∀ SchemaText • Predicate
                    | Predicate1
Predicate1::=       className.INIT
                    | pre operationName
                    | operationName
                    | relationName
                    | Predicate1 ∧ Predicate1
                    | Predicate1 ⇒ Predicate1
                    | (Predicate)
SchemaText::=       className.STATE [Decoration]
className::=        Word
operationName::=    className.Word
relationName::=     Word [Decoration]
Word                category for undecorated names
Decoration::=       '
```

Definition for the Transformation:

This section contains the specification of function T that takes a refinement condition written in Object-Z and returns the corresponding refinement condition written in OCL. Function T is applied in the context of a UML model **M** containing all the elements which are referred to in the Z expressions. Apart from producing an OclExpression, function T returns an OclFile containing additional definitions that are created during the transformation.

UML elements are retrieved form **M** by using standard lookup operations on its environment as it is defined in [16].

T : Model -> Predicate -> (OclExpression, OclFile)

T_M(Predicate1 $\land$ Predicate2)= (e,Φ)

    Where

    T_M(Predicate1)= (e1, Φ1)

    T_M(Predicate2)= (e2, Φ2)

    e= e1 **"and"** e2

    Φ = Φ1 *merge* Φ2

T_M(Predicate1 $\Rightarrow$ Predicate2)= (e,Φ)

    Where

    T_M(Predicate1)= (e1, Φ1)

    T_M(Predicate2)= (e2, Φ2)

    e= e1 **"implies"** e2

    Φ = Φ1 *merge* Φ2

T_M($\forall$ className.**STATE** • Predicate) = (e,Φ)

    Where

    T_M(Predicate)= (e1, Φ)

    e=className".allInstances()->forAll
    ("iteratorName"|"e1")"

    iteratorName= toLowerCase(className)

T_M($\forall$ className.**STATE'** • Predicate) = (e,Φ)

    Where

    T_M(Predicate)= (e1, Φ)

    e=className".allInstances()->forAll
    ("iteratorName"|"e1")"

    iteratorName= toLowerCase(className) "_post"

T_M($\exists$ className.**STATE** • Predicate) = (e,Φ)

    Where

T_M(Predicate)= (e1, Φ)

e=className".allInstances()->exists
("iteratorName"|"e1")"

iteratorName= toLowerCase(className)

T_M($\exists$ className.**STATE'** • Predicate) = (e,Φ)

Where

T_M(Predicate)= (e1, Φ)

e=className".allInstances()-
>exists("iteratorName"|"e1")"

iteratorName= toLowerCase(className) "_post"

T_M (className.*INIT*) =(e,Φ)

Where

e= toLowerCase(className) ".isInit()"

Φ = **"Package"** packageName
   "context" className **"def:** isInit(): Boolean ="

propertyName$_1$"="exp$_1$"**and**"..."**and**"propertyName$_n$"="exp$_n$
   "**endPackage**"

Where

packageName = class.package.name

class=M.getEnvironmentWithParents().lookup(className)

Properties = class.allProperties()->select
(p|p.initialValue->notEmpty())

$\forall$j•1≤j≤properties->size()•
   propertyName$_j$ = properties->at(j).name
   exp$_j$ = properties->at(j).initialValue.body

T_M(**pre** className.operationName) = (e, $\varnothing$)[1]

Where:

e = operation.precondition.specification.body

Where:

operation : UMLOperation =
   M.getEnvironmentWithParents().lookup(className).
   getEnvironmentWithParents()
   .lookupImplicitOperation(operationName, Sequence{})

T_M (className.operationName)= (e, $\varnothing$)

Where:

---

[1] In this document the symbol $\varnothing$ is an abbreviation denoting the empty package.

```
e =
operation.postcondition.specification.body.renamed()
```
Where:
```
operation : UMLOperation   =
   M.getEnvironmentWithParents().lookup(className).
   getEnvironmentWithParents()
    .lookupImplicitOperation(operationName,Sequence{})
```
Where:

function renamed() is applied on an OclExpression returning a copy of the expression where any undecorated name v has been renamed as v_post and any decorated name v@pre has been renamed as v.

T_M (relationName) = (e, Φ)

Where:

```
relationName ∈ Word -- it is an undecorated name
e = absInstance ".mapping(" refInstance ")"
```
Φ = **"Package"** packageName
```
   "Context" absInstance ":" AbstractClass   "def:"
   "mapping("refInstance":"RefinedClass ")":Boolean ="
exp    "endPackage"
```
Where:
```
packageName = d.package.name
d : Abstraction =
M.getEnvironmentWithParents().lookup(relationName)
AbstractClass  = d.supplier.name
RefinedClass = d.client.name
absInstance = toLowerCase(AbstractClass)
refInstance = toLowerCase(RefinedClass)
exp = d.mapping.body
```
T_M (relationName') = $(e, \emptyset)$

Where:
```
e = absInstance ".mapping(" refInstance ")"
```
Where:
```
d : Abstraction =
M.getEnvironmentWithParents().lookup(relationName)
AbstractClass  = d.supplier.name
RefinedClass = d.client.name
absInstance = toLowerCase(AbstractClass) "_post"
refInstance = toLowerCase(RefinedClass)  "_post"
```

A cognitive model of user interaction as a guideline for designing novel interfaces

Felipe Aguilera[1], Rosa A. Alarcón[2], Luis A. Guerrero[1], César A. Collazos[3]

[1] Department of Computer Science, Universidad de Chile
Av. Blanco Encalada 2120, Santiago, Chile
{faguiler, luguerre}@dcc.uchile.cl

[2] Department of Computer Science,
Pontificia Universidad Católica de Chile.
Av. Vicuña Mackenna 4860, 6904411, Santiago Chile.
ralarcon@ing.puc.cl

[3] System Department, Universidad del Cauca
FIET, Sector Tulcan, Popayán-Colombia
ccollazo@unicauca.edu.co

Abstract. Adaptive systems behavior based on user models appear promising, mostly for complex environments such as mixed reality environments (MRE). An MRE comprises a virtual representation of the reality as well as physical objects augmented with virtual features. These objects are coupled with the virtual representation so that they can reflect its changes in real time. The proper design of an MRE and the user models that it implies are crucial for its success, but unfortunately, there are no guidelines for the design of these environments. In this paper we present a methodology for designing user models for MRE as well as for the augmentation of physical everyday objects. The user model describes users' knowledge in two levels of abstraction: objects manipulation (syntax) and its meaning assigned by a community of practice (semantics).

1 Introduction

User models could be defined as models that a system have about users, which reside inside the computational environment. An advantage of this approach is that a system can adapt itself to the current task or user, dynamically and with little effort or none required from the user [6]. This property is interesting mostly in complex

Please use the following format when citing this chapter:

Aguilera, F., Alarcón, R.A., Guerrero, L.A., Collazos, C.A., 2006, in IFIP International Federation for Information Processing, Volume 219, Advanced Software Engineering: Expanding the Frontiers of Software Technology, eds. Ochoa, S., Roman, G.-C., (Boston: Springer), pp. 62–76.

environments such as mixed reality environments (from now on MRE). MREs blend the real and the virtual [19] by keeping virtual representations of real things and introducing virtual features in the real world through complex objects. A complex object has a real concrete part coupled to various virtual representations (simulation, animation, symbolic) by means of grasp or image recognition [3].

Although research in MRE [15, 18, 22], tangible user interfaces (TUI) [9, 12], and multimodal interfaces [14], look promising, they cannot be considered by default beneficial. Bad designs lead to unnatural interfaces, hard to understand, requiring an extra cognitive effort from users [20], for manipulate them (syntax), and understanding the results of such manipulation (semantics). Unfortunately, most experiences reported in TUIs and MREs, are mainly ad hoc design strategies [14] instead of the general design frameworks of GUI interfaces research [16]. In addition, research in novel interfaces does not consider real contexts of use. As a result, there is not a clear understanding of users' needs, restrictions, knowledge and assumptions in relation with the interface. This situation avoids making a proper evaluation of interfaces impact on users and many times "hammers in search of nails" are created. For the case of user models in MREs, this situation is challenging because if the system decides to adapt itself according to a misconceived user model the resulting action could be performed in the physical world of a user and turn into a odd action.

How can we identify the most important aspects to consider when designing an MRE?. A first notion could be "transparent artifacts", it states that a well-designed artifact (such as a door) becomes transparent when it is used: it allows us to focus on the task at hand instead of on the artifact itself (e.g. a door allows us to focus on our plans such as getting into the kitchen instead of on the door itself) [1]. This concept is used in GUI interfaces design: it exploit users' knowledge about the world such as pointing, grabbing and moving objects [22]. Such knowledge can be understood as the perceived objects' properties in order to manipulate them or affordances (e.g. a file can be grasp through a hand icon) [8], and the expected results (e.g. erase a file).

But users' knowledge about artifacts goes beyond its physical manipulation; users assign meaning to objects based also on its use [1]. For instance, GUI designers facilitate the users' understanding of its actions, by exploiting common knowledge and organizing GUI elements into metaphors (e.g. providing a trashcan icon for files deletion). Particularly, *everyday objects* (EO) such as keys, doors, rooms, etc. have a meaning shared by a specific community. Users have expectations about them: a lawyer may expect to find his office door closed, while students may expect to find their room door opened. Just as we use basic knowledge such as pointing, grabbing, etc, and semantic knowledge such as metaphors in GUI interfaces, we can exploit EOs semantics for creating MREs with user models encapsulating this knowledge so that the system can adapt itself without disturbing the user.

In this paper, we present a methodology for guiding the design of a cognitive user model in order to enrich EOs comprised by a MRE. Our methodology has three main tasks: *syntax modeling*, which consists of characterizing EO manipulation (e.g. grabbing); *praxis modeling*, which consists of identifying the shared meaning assigned by a community to the EO; and *object augmentation*, which consists of determining the new virtual features of the object and its impact on the original object's syntax and semantics.

The resulting MRE comprehends a virtual representation of the real world, a set of complex objects immersed in the users' real world and a set of user cognitive models (one for each user). A *user model* encapsulates the user knowledge and assumptions about complex objects at two levels of complexity: its manipulation or syntax (grasping, moving, etc.), and the semantics associated with its *use* in a determined context [1]. As an example, we used our methodology for guiding the design of a MRE called "Collaborative Virtual-Real Environment" or CVRE [7, 10]. CVRE includes a virtual representation of the real facilities of our Department of Computer Science at University of Chile, a set of complex objects (the real part is coupled with the virtual by means of grasp recognition) and a set of user models implemented through software agents.

The rest of the paper is organized as follows: section 2 describes the conceptual background of our methodology. Section 3 shows the proposed cognitive user model for MREs. In section 4 we present the use of our methodology in a practical example. In section 5 we describe our CVRE. Finally, section 6 presents some conclusions.

2   Contextual knowledge: syntax and semantics

In the area of context-aware computing, user context is described as the conditions associated to the user's current location, such as: social aspects [5], physical properties [12] or related information [4]. More generally, *context* can be understood as "*the interrelated conditions in which an event, action, etc. takes place*"[1]. In Artificial Intelligence (AI), context is used for *interpreting* the meaning of a sentence. For instance, if a friend asks us to "close the window", in a *cold, windy day*, we may understand that s/he refers to a physical window instead of a MS-Window. This way, context narrows down the proper interpretation of an expression [2]. In groupware, contextual information is provided to group members so they can *understand* how their actions fit into the group goals and choose the appropriate response among a set of possibilities [21]. In all these scenarios, context is used to determine the meaning of a situation, a sentence or an action, so that an appropriate response can be built.

In HCI, Bannon [1] proposes that objects should not be studied only as "things". Objects have no meaning in isolation: they are given meaning only through their incorporation into social praxis. This way, objects' meaning depends on the *context of use* of such object. We define this context as "the interrelated conditions in which an individual interact *purposely* with such object". Such conditions can be differentiated at least in two complexity levels: the manipulation or actions performed by users on the object (*syntax*) and the interpretation of its results or consequences (*semantics*).

According to Bannon, this semantics would depend on the community who uses the object. For instance, a regular family uses a frigidaire to store food, but in a hospital (another context of use), people can use frigidaires to store blood samples.

---

[1] Excerpt from Merriam Webster On Line at http: // www.m-w.com .

In that way, communities determine different contexts of use and meaning for objects. The objects and their manipulation may be the same (syntax), but users' knowledge about the results of their manipulation depends on the context of use.

Others, like Brezillon [2] considers that contextual knowledge has two aspects: static knowledge, which remains constant throughout the interaction; and dynamic knowledge that changes throughout the interaction. Consider for example, an everyday object such as a pencil. The knowledge associated to its manipulation (e.g. how to hold a pencil) is mainly static and can be used in diverse contexts (e.g. grading students test, setting appointments in a PDA touch screen, etc.), however, when used it may serve to draw lines or to pick up a file (e.g. in the touch screen), the dynamic nature of context serves as a mean for supporting users' diverse goal or to allow users to assign unexpected uses to objects.

Finally, a fundamental guide for understanding the knowledge associated to the functioning of objects from a cognitive point of view, is provided by Norman [17]. He defines a series of concepts such as affordances (the perceived properties of a thing that determine how it could possibly be used), constraints (the perceived properties of a thing that prohibits some activities and encourages others), feedback (the perceived properties of a thing that permits sending information to users about what action has been done), etc.

Objects allow to share and divide work practice among people, mediating the people' work. This is particularly important in groupware where a well-designed shared object can help users to understand their work and choose a proper behavior, providing a better collaboration scenario. When people share a common physical space but interact in an asynchronous way objects become the elements through which people leave traces of their actions and intentions. In all these cases people' actions on objects are interpreted in the context of use that the particular worker's community shares and allows them to coordinate their actions.

2.1 Dimensions for Analysis and Design

Norman's concepts are useful for describing an object manipulation, but they are too general. With the aim of obtaining more specific guidelines, we followed Gutwin's and Greenberg's strategy [11]. They used five "type of questions" iteratively (what, who, when, how, where), for defining some dimensions of analysis and modeling of groupware context (e.g. identity, location, etc). After some iterations, refinement and discussion we found some useful dimensions for MREs. They are: Usage, Feedback, History, Intention, Consequence, Action, Dependence, Opportunity, Access, Roles, Reach and View. Each dimension must be defined in the two levels of abstraction discussed previously: syntactic (manipulation) and semantic (interpretation of manipulation by a community) level.

Usage: When referred to syntax, it describes the mechanism for manipulating an object. It could be obtained by answering a "How" question: e.g. How do you manipulate a key? (related to Norman's affordance concept, as well).

Feedback: When referred to syntax, it describes the mechanism to know when an action has been done. It could be obtained by answering "How" questions: e.g. How do you know the consequences of using a key? (Norman's feedback concept).

History: When referred to syntax, it provides information about past events concerning presence, location or action. It could be obtained by answering "Who" questions: e.g. Who used a key?, "Where": e.g. Where is the person that used a key?, and "How": e.g. How do you know if a key was used (Norman's constraints concept).

Intention: When referred to syntax, it describes the object properties that a user expects to change when interacting with the object. It could be obtained by answering "What" questions: e.g. What is a key used for? (Norman's affordance concept). When referred to semantics, intention describes the meaning associated to an object property change. It could be obtained by answering the question "What": e.g. "What is the user intention when using a key?".

Consequence: When referred to syntax, it gives information about the actions the user can predict when perform an action over an artifact. It could be obtained by answering "What" questions: e.g. What is the direct consequence of use a key?

Action: When referred to syntax, this aspect provides information about the state or process of doing something. It could be obtained by answering "What" questions: e.g. What do I do with a key?

Dependence: When referred to syntax, it describes the state of being determined, influenced, or controlled by something else. It could be obtained by answering "What" questions: e.g. What is the dependence of a key with people?

Opportunity: When referred to syntax, it represents favorable or advantageous circumstance or combination of circumstances of doing something. It could be obtained by answering "When" questions: e.g. When is a key used?

Access: When referred to syntax, it indicates the permissions of the people of use certain artifacts. It could be obtained by answering "Who" questions: e.g. Who can use a key?

Roles: When referred to syntax, it presents the characteristic and expected social behavior of an individual. It could be obtained by answering "Who" questions: e.g. Who should use a key?

Reach: When refereed to syntax, it describes what is reached when an object is used. It could be obtained by answering "Where" questions: e.g. Where does a key allow to reach?

View: When refereed to syntax, it describes what is viewed when an object is used. It could be obtained by answering "Where" questions: e.g. Where does a key allow to view?

3   Cognitive User Model for Designing Mixed Reality

In this section, we present a methodology for designing adaptive MREs. It comprehends five steps implemented in three phases: everyday objects syntax modeling, praxis modeling, and augmenting objects.

3.1   Phase 1: Everyday objects syntax modeling

Our aim is to design MREs that include everyday objects augmented with virtual features. By augment, we mean to manipulate a physical artifact so that it is publicly, and in most cases permanently, recognized to represent or denote something else. This kind of natural augmentation is an activity that human beings perform constantly. Our first step is to determine which objects will be considered as part of the environment. One of the risks when augmenting objects with new functionality is that we distort objects' syntax and semantics in a way that we lose useful properties or change the object so much that users may need extra cognitive effort to use it.

In order to avoid this, we model the object real syntax (manipulation) and semantics (interpretation) using the dimensions described in section 2.1 (numbered circles 1 and 2 in fig, 1). In this way, we can perform later a controlled distortion.

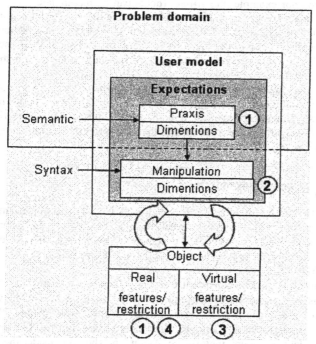

Fig. 1. An outline of the methodology followed for augmenting objects. A user cognitive model about an artifact comprising syntactic and semantic aspects is initially created. The model is used as a basis for performing a progressive and controlled distortion of the object.

3.2   Phase 2: Praxis modeling

Diverse communities will assign different meaning to the same object: for instance in a university, if an aula door is left half-opened, one may expect that students will get in as they arrive; however, if the door belongs to a lawyer office, one may interpret it as a potential security hazard. Furthermore, within a community we can find different types of users or roles, such as teachers, secretaries, students, etc., whose praxis may be slightly different for each one.

A first step is to identify the set of users or roles in a community. For each of them, we must characterize their knowledge about objects usage. Again we use our dimensions for finding objects semantics (numbered circle 3 in fig. 1). In figure 1 we can observe that syntax and semantics are separated with a dotted line. Indeed, we can see that semantics are included in a box labeled "problem domain". This is because syntax or manipulation can be the same across diverse domains of use, for instance in the door example, the artifact (door) can be manipulated with the same set of actions in a school or in a lawyer office (assume that the object manipulated is the same). The opposite applies for shared meaning of object manipulation; diverse communities will assign another meaning to them, depending of their use context. For instance lawyers and teachers could assign different meanings for a structurally similar half-opened door.

Semantics may be expressed as shared policies: users of a certain type agree on a specific interpretation of objects usage and needs. For instance, secretaries may agree that the doors of their offices must remain opened during their work-time. This knowledge corresponds to the assumptions that the system takes into consideration when adapting its behavior.

3.3   Phase 3: Augmenting objects

The goal of the phases previously presented is to identify the objects in order to augment, their physical properties, weaken their restrictions and manipulation constraints, as well as to change the expectations hold by each type of user in relation with each object. In this stage, we define the desired objects' virtual features (numbered circle 4 in fig. 1).

These features should be consistent with the syntax and semantics defined in the previous steps. A designer may choose to change some of them, but s/he will know in advance that users may need to learn how to use these new features. As well, a designer may choose to modify an object (numbered circle 5 in fig. 1). For instance, s/he could add leds, speakers, motors, etc. Again s/he should consider the impact of his/her choice on syntax and semantics. If the object is modified, then its physical constrains and manipulation could change. Furthermore, users may decide to change their shared policies in order to take advantage of objects new possibilities. In this case the cycle must be followed again (cyclic arrows in fig. 1).

In the next section we apply our methodology for creating a MRE. The environment comprises the physical workplace of the Computer Science Department at the University of Chile that has a counterpart in the virtual world in the form of a

Web based Collaborative Virtual Environment. Additionally, physical elements such as doors, keys and rooms have been augmented following the methodology.

4   Designing a CVRE

In a previous work we have designed a Collaborative Virtual Environment (CVE) [10], which is a virtual space where people can collaborate. The CVE visually mimics the real world in order that people can use it in a natural way. Now we will extend our previous work and transform it into a MRE (CVRE) comprising augmented everyday objects.

4.1   Everyday objects syntax modeling.

The everyday objects considered as part of our CVRE are rooms [10], doors, door-locks and keys. Rooms are virtual representation of the real workplaces in the Computer Science Department: X teachers' offices, Y students' rooms, etc. Rooms are assigned to one people (owner). Access to rooms is controlled by one wood door without glasses and one door-lock. Door keys are assigned to room owners. The administrator keeps also a copy of each key. A properties summary is shown in Table 1.

Table 1. . Our CVE contains rooms, doors with locks and keys. Their real features are described in this table

Room	Door	Lock	Key
- workspace: academic office, secretary office, aula room, meeting room, etc.	- it allows to the enter into a room.	- it allows to close a door.	- it allows to leave closed a lock.
•	- it can be open, semi-open or closed.	- it is used with a key- equal locks are allowed.	- we can obtain a key copy.
- it can have glass walls (transparent) or not.			- is transferable.
- assigned to 1 or more people.	- it can have glass walls (transparent) or not.		- it is possible to be taken to all parts.
- it has a door.	- it has a lock.		

4.2   Praxis modeling

CVRE users are: Professors, Administrative personnel, Research assistants, Teaching assistants, Students and other academic personnel. In table 2 we present the praxis modeling for Professors in relation with an office door.

Table 2. Praxis model of a door office. The table shows the detailed analysis of the shared meaning assigned by teachers to their doors. The user model will contain some of these dimensions as rules used to adapt CVE to users preferences. Notice that at the semantic level, teachers' offices or rooms are workspaces.

Dimension	Question	Answer (Door)
History	How do you know if a door was used?	If either the door status, the workspace content or the workspace status has changed since last visit.
Intention	What is the objective to open a door?	To enter into a closed workspace. To change the visibility of a workspace. To allow that some person leaves the workspace. To allow people to inspect workspace content.
	What is the objective to close a door?	To close an opened workspace. To change the visibility of a workspace. To avoid others to leaves the workspace. To avoid others to inspect the contents of a workspace.
Consequence	What is the direct consequence of keep the door opened?	Passers-by can contact people inside the workspace. Workspace contents are visible for everybody. A person is allowed to leave the office.
	What is the direct consequence of keep the door closed?	Hide the content of the workspace. Users must knock the door, for knowing if anybody is inside. We do not know who is outside room.
Action	What do you do with a door?	Enter / leave a workspace. Allow / deny the visibility of the workspace contents.
Dependence	What is the dependency with people?	Regularly, people who open a door, have sufficient permissions to enter into the workspace.
Opportunity	When is a door used?	When a user needs to enter/leave a workspace. When a user needs that other people enter/leave workspace.
Access	Who can use a door?	The person who are next to a door and need to open/close it.
Roles	Who should use a door?	The person who is allowed to open/close it.

In table 3 we present an analysis of the syntax modeling of a key. Note the differences with table 2: the answers are described in terms of physical properties and not in terms of the changes that we performed.

Table 3. Syntax model for a door office key. The table shows the detailed analysis for understanding key manipulation. Possible key status will be also contained in the user model.

Dimension	Question	Answer (Key)
Usage	How do you manipulate a key?	Putting the key in the door lock.
Feedback	How do you know that it is the correct key	Because the key fits the door lock. If it does not, it is not the correct key.
History	How do you know if a key was used?	I cannot be sure.
Intention	What is a key used for?	Opening/closing door locks.
Consequence	What is the direct consequence of using a key?	Door locks change their state to open/close.
Action	What do you do with a key?	Putting the key in the door lock, turning it, and removing the key.
Dependence	What is the dependency with peoples?	Only the carrier of the key can use it.
	What is the dependency with door-locks?	Only the key that fits the door lock can be used.
Opportunity	When is a key used?	When I have the key that fits a door lock and I want to open/close the door of a room.
Access	Who can use a key?	The people that have a key.
Roles	Who should use a key?	People that have a key and need to open the a door lock.
View	Where does a key allow to view?	The contents of the room associated with a door related with a key (transitive).
Reach	Where does a key allow to reach?	To the room associated with the key.
History	Where is the person that used the key?	Possibly in the room, but I cannot be sure.

4.3   Augmenting objects

Table 4 describes the virtual features that we have chosen for augmenting some objects. The most important feature is the creation of a desktop-lock, which is basically a door-look that allows us to open and close virtual shared workplaces by using an augmented key. Unlike the real world, desktop-locks are not associated with just one key, but with many keys as long as they belong to a valid virtual workplace.

Table 4. . Virtual features of rooms, doors with locks and keys, chosen according properties discovered in tables 2 and 3

Room	Door	Lock	Key
virtual workspaces	new intermediate state: semi-opened door. (which define a semi-accessible space)	desktop lock: allows to open and close virtual shared workplaces. We can use the same lock for various rooms (only change the keys)	activity log (register past event about use of a key)

5   Implementing the CVRE

We have used phidgets for augmenting everyday objects (e.g. the key-lock pair). Phidgets (physical widgets) are specialized devices developed at the University of Calgary that leverages the complexities of developing physical interfaces [9]. The philosophy behind Phidgets is to resemble the GUI widgets; they are GUI elements that encapsulate interface interaction and make GUIs easy to develop as they may be arranged for composing an application interface. Phidgets encapsulates minimal functionality for rapid prototyping of physical interfaces. The elements we have used for implementing our CVRE are: a Phidget Interface Kit (the main interface where all the sensors are connected to); a rotation sensor (which allows us to control the twists of the key in the lock); three LEDs (allowing us to give feedback about the accessibility state provided by the key); a RFID (Radio frequency identification, a small object attached to a key that allows us to read information associated with each key in order to identify them); a movement sensor (that allows us to know if the user leaves his keys in the lock at the time of leaving his job). Fig. 2a depicts the augmented interface built.

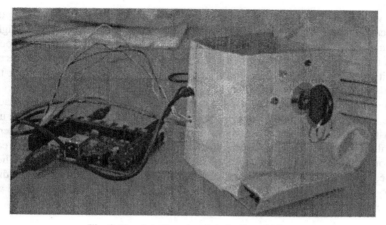

Fig. 2. Key interface developed using phidgets

Three LEDs (a red, green and yellow ones), indicate the accessibility provided for a particular room. The green color represents a totally opened lock (a fully accessible space); the red color represents a closed lock (a totally inaccessible space), and the yellow color represents the intermediate state previously described (a semi-accessible space). A tag has been attached to each key, so that it makes possible to the RFID reader to identify and differentiate the used keys. For this reason, it is necessary that the keys associated with different virtual rooms be physically equal (in order to be accepted by the regular lock). The tags attached to them differentiate keys.

A movement sensor is located next to the lock, facing the user (the white circle on fig.2a), in order to detect his/her presence or absence.

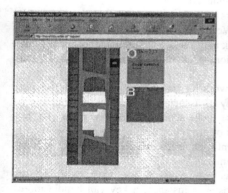
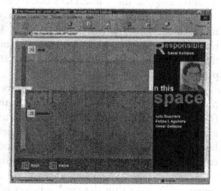

Fig. 3. CVE main interface corresponds with the floor plan of DCC. Keys are used to allows a user to access his or her personal space

CVE virtual rooms. Our CVE [7] maps the real physical design of our Computer Science Department and allow CVE users to be aware of such structure through a floor map (Fig. 2b and 2c). Users can access into their own personal space (a room) or get into the virtual workspace of a colleague. Again we follow our guidelines and exploit the knowledge that users have about the structure and division of work that actually occurs at our Computer Science Department.

In our CVE, users employ the desktop-key to open and close virtual spaces. Doors allow users to control their privacy and the degree of availability that a user wants that by-passers perceive about him. Our key-lock interface allows a user to control the state that the user wishes others to see in the virtual interface. For it, each position of the key corresponds to a state: totally closed (red) to indicate that s/he is offline, totally opened (green) to indicate that s/he is available, and an intermediate state (yellow) to indicate that one is busy or temporarily absent. This alternative was used to control the state of a user of a session of instant message.

6   Conclusions and Further Work

The presented work stresses out the importance of the design of physical interfaces that take into account the previous users' knowledge about the objects' context of use. Such context comprises both syntactic and semantic categories of analysis. There has been a large tradition of discontinuity between the rich interactions with objects in our physical world, and the impoverished interactions with electronic material. The linkage between these two worlds has been difficult and expensive. But we believe that rather than force users to adopt radical forms of interaction, we may exploit instead the achieved knowledge about how the world works. By augmenting pre-existing tools within the framework of a work praxis or context of use, we may bring computing to the world instead of the other way around. By designing interfaces that augment objects' features, but keeping a coherent semantics with the original version and its usage in the real world, we believe that a more natural design of these interfaces could be achieved.

On the other hand, computing nowadays provides enormous potential for novel, unexpected, rich and useful interaction. We do not argue against such approach, however, we believe that the presented work may serve as a reference for identifying the successful design choices and its rationale as well as to suggest needs and promising research areas.

In this paper we have presented a framework for analyzing the context of use of a physical everyday object in order to identify its associated semantics, augmenting it (i.e. by adding intermediate states) and use those semantics for new tasks (i.e. by allowing to handle multiple context of work or providing availability awareness). We have used phidgets as a medium for ugmenting and manipulating everyday objects easily (i.e. a key as an authentication mechanism).

Other issues we want to explore as future work, are the possibility of dynamically selecting devices' relationships. For instance, a key can handle more than one application, but the lock is physically the same for each door. Hence, we want to explore the possibility to enrich the key so that it can provide multi sensory information (i.e. change its color), so that a key may represent indeed a set of keys. May the users perform a context switch because of the color? The research question for further work aims to identify more context attributes. For instance we may argue that users' intention when manipulating an object actually triggers the users' appropriate context for interpreting, let us say, an action. Otherwise, physical (sensory) arrangement of physical environment may trigger users' appropriate interpretation context.

Finally in order to answer the questions raised in the discussion as well as to learn more on the effects of this approach on users, we need to design appropriate tests and evaluate the objects' usage in varios context of use.

References

1. Bannon L., Bødker S.: Beyond the interface: Encountering artifacts in use. In: J. Carroll (ed.): Designing Interaction: Psychology at the Human-Computer Interface. Cambridge: Cambridge University Press 1991, pp. 227-253.
2. Brézillon, P. and Abu-Hakima, S.: Using knowledge in its context: Report on the IJCAI-93 Workshop. The AI Magazine, 1995, 16(1), pp. 87-91.
3. Bruns, F. W.: Complex Objects and Anthropocentric Systems Design. In: Advances in Networked Enterprises (L. M. Camarinha-Matos, H. Afsarmanesh, H.-H. Erbe (Eds.), Boston, 2000, pp.249-258.
4. Cheverst, K., Davies, N., Mitchell, K., Friday, A., Efstratiou, C.: Developing a context-aware electronic tourist guide: some issues and experiences. CHI'00, pp. 17-24.
5. Dey, A. K., Salber, D., Abowd, G. D.: A Conceptual Framework and a Toolkit for Supporting the Rapid Prototyping of Context-Aware Applications. In Moran, T.P. and Dourish, P. (Eds.) Context-Aware Computing: A Special Triple Issue of Human-Computer Interaction. Lawrence-Erlbaum, March 2002.
6. Fischer G.: User Modeling in Human-Computer Interaction, In User Modeling and User-Adapted Interaction, UMUAI,, 11(1), 2001, pp. 65-86.
7. Frecon, E., and Nou A.: Building distributed virtual environments to support collaborative work. ACM Symposium on Virtual Reality Software and Technology, VRST'98, pp.105-113, Taipei, Taiwan, Nov. 1998.
8. Gibson, J. J.: The theory of affordances. In R. E. Shaw and J. Bransford (Eds.), Perceiving, Acting, and Knowing. Hillsdale, NJ: Lawrence Erlbaum Associates, 1977.
9. Greenberg, S., and Fitchett, C.: Phidgets: Easy development of physical interfaces through physical widgets. Proceedings of the ACM UIST 2001 Symposium on User Interface Software and Technology, November, Orlando, Florida, ACM Press, 2001.
10. Guerrero, L. A., Collazos, C. A., Pino J. A., Ochoa S. F., and Aguilera, F.: Designing Virtual Environments to Support Collaborative Work in Real Spaces, Journal of Web Engineering, 2(4), October, 2004, pp.282-294.
11. Gutwin, C. and Greenberg, S.: A Descriptive Framework of Workspace Awareness for Real-Time Groupware. Computer Supported Cooperative Work, 11(3-4), 411-446, Special Issue on Awareness in CSCW, Kluwer Academic Press, 2002.
12. Ishii, H., and Ulmer, B., Tangible bits: Towards seamless interfaces between people, bits and atoms. Proceedings of the ACM CHI'97, pp. 234-241, 1997.
13. Leech, G.: Semantics: The Study of Meaning. Harmondsworth, UK: Penguin, (1981).

14. MacLean, K. E. and Roderick J. B.: Smart Tangible Displays in the Everyday World: a Haptic Door Knob. Proceedings of the IEEE/ASME International Conference on Advanced Intelligent Mechatronics, AIM'99, September 1999, Atlanta, USA.
15. McGee, D.R., Cohen, P.: Creating Tangible Interfaces by Augmenting Physical Objects with Multimodal Language. Intelligent User Interfaces, 2001, pp.113-119.
16. Nielsen, J.: Usability Engineering. The Computer Science and Engineering Handbook 1997, pp. 1440-1460.
17. Norman, D. A.: The Design of Everyday Things, London/New York: MIT Press, 2000.
18. Olwal, A. and Feiner S.: The Flexible Pointer: An Interaction Technique for Augmented and Virtual Reality, UIST 2003, Vancouver, BC, November 2003, pp. 81-82.
19. Ohta, Y., Tamura, H.: Mixed Reality–Merging Real and Virtual Worlds. Tokyo, 1999.
20. Shneiderman, B.: Direct Manipulation for Comprehensible, Predictable and Controllable User Interfaces. Proceedings of International User Interfaces, 1997, pp. 33-39.
21. Sohlenkamp, M.: Supporting group awareness in Multi-User Environments through Perceptualization. GMD Research Series, No.6 Zugl.: Padderborn, Univ. Diss, 1999.
22. Want, R., Fishkin, K.P., Gujar, A., and Harrison, B.L.: Bridging physical and virtual worlds with electronic tags. Proceedings of the Conference on Human Factors in Computing Systems, 1999, ACM Press, pp.370-377.

An empirical evaluation for business process tools

Erika M. Nieto-Ariza[1], Guillermo Rodríguez-Ortiz[1,2], Javier Ortiz-Hernández[1]

1 Centro Nacional de Investigación y Desarrollo Tecnológico,
Interior internado Palmira s/n, Cuernavaca, Morelos, 62490 México
{erika, ortiz}@ cenidet.edu.mx
Home page: http://www.cenidet.edu.mx
2 Instituto de Investigaciones Eléctricas, Reforma 113, 62490,
Cuernavaca, Morelos, 62490, México
gro@iie.org.mx

Abstract. As the use of web grows, organizations are increasingly choosing to use it to provide their services. The modeling process is a previous step in the systematization of a process. Due to the great number of modeling tools in existence, it is necessary to identify the information that tools allow to specify. A set of concepts is proposed to evaluate modeling tools using three levels of abstractions. The proposal compares the modeling capabilities supplied by the different techniques and allows determining what modeling tool is the most appropriate to model specific concepts of interest to a problem.

1 Introduction

Models are commonly used to represent complex systems and to observe the performance in the business process when a technology system is integrated. Technology systems should support business and they become an integral part of the business process [1,2,3,4,5]. Due to the great number of techniques to model and specify requirements, it is complex and laborious to compare them. Three modeling levels are proposed which integrate a set of concepts to build web application models: a) Organizational, its goal is to describe how the organization works and the business process that are going to be systematized with a web information system; b) Conceptual, its goal is to describe the role of the software system and its integration with a particular organizational environment; c) Web, its goal is to describe the semantics of a web application [5,6]. The basis of our contribution is in the detection and classification of a set of concepts which are used to analyze, to evaluate modeling tools and to recognize the capabilities that each tool has in order to model at the three levels of abstraction.

Please use the following format when citing this chapter:

Nieto-Ariza, E.M., Rodriguez-Ortiz, G., Ortiz-Hernández, J., 2006, in IFIP International Federation for Information Processing, Volume 219, Advanced Software Engineering: Expanding the Frontiers of Software Technology, eds. Ochoa, S., Roman, G.-C., (Boston: Springer), pp. 77–84.

There are some methods and methodologies to evaluate business process modeling, but they evaluate the functionality of an application or a modeling tool. Rosemman proposes an ontology to evaluate organizational modeling grammars identifying their strength and weaknesses [7]. Luis Olsina and Devanshu Dhyani [8, 9] propose a methodology to evaluate the characteristics of a web application in operational phases. The structure of this paper is as follows: in section 2 the modeling concepts that comprise our approach are presented, in section 3 the modeling concepts are enhanced with a set of aspects found to be useful in building models, in section 4 the evaluation results are presented, in section 5 a product evaluation is presented, last the conclusions are discussed.

2 Modeling concepts

A business process model can be viewed at many levels of abstraction, and complementary model views can be combined to give a more intelligible, accurate view of a system to develop than a single model alone [3]. This approach establishes three levels of abstraction and each one includes certain modeling concepts of features (table 1). Concepts are properties or characteristics that structurally describe types of requirements and define the key elements in a business process. The concepts facilitate integration of the levels of abstraction, such that, starting with an organizational model, the elements of the conceptual and the web model are easily identified. The selection of the concepts is a task that requires the analysis of different modeling tools. Through the correspondence of an concept in one level to its corresponding concept in the next level, the three levels are integrated in a complete view of the business process. For example, the task concept in the organizational level correspond to the functional concept at the conceptual level and later it will be correspond to an event concept at the Web level of abstraction.

Table 1. Modeling concepts at each level of abstraction

Organizational level	Conceptual level	Web level	
		Business process	Pure navigation
Actor	Actor	---	Navigation page – Relationship
		User profile (Rol)	User profile (Rol)
		Class (objetct)	---
Resource	Artifact		
		Artifact	Artifact
Goal	Goal	---	Objective
Task	Function	Service	Service
Activity	Event		
		Event	---
Business rule	Constraint	Pre and post condition	---
Quality	No functional requirement	No functional requirement	---

The **organizational** modeling concepts are as follows.
- *Goal*. It describes a business process desired state that an organization imposes to itself, with a certain degree of priority; the goal must be quantified whenever possible.
- *Actor*. It describes an entity that has a specific goal, participates in the business process, or has relationships with other actors. An actor may have different roles.
todo- *Resource*. It describes an informational or physical entity that is transferred between actors as a result of task executed by an actor.
- *Task*. It describes a series of activities oriented to reach a goal; it may indicate how should be accomplished.
- *Activity*. It describes a set of actions to carry out one task.
- *Quality*. It describes the desired characteristics in the business process.
- *Business rule*. It describes the actions and criteria that govern the execution of the business process.

The **conceptual** modeling concepts are as follows.
- *Goal*. It describes the information system purpose, limitations and responsibilities, from the business view point.
-*Actor*. It describes an entity (human, hardware, software or process activity) that interacts with the information system and that might play different roles.
- *Artifact*. It describes an abstract or physical entity that is transferred between an actor and the information system.
- *Function*. It describes a service that must be provided by the system to the actors.
- *Event*. It describes a change in the business process in one instant specific of time.
- *Non functional*. It describes the desired quality features or constraints for the information system as for example, platform and interface requirements, etc.
- *Constraint*. It describes a condition for a service execution provide by the system.

The **Web** modeling concepts are as follows.
- *Objective*. The purpose of the Web application, from a simple information pages displayer to a complex and sophisticated corporate portal.
- *Navigation relationship*. It describes a global vision of the Web application according to a user profile with relation to the information to be presented.
- *User profile*. It describes the user unique use of the Web application. A user can have many profiles for the same Web application.
- *Class*. It describes an object type to model the entities that integrate the application, and the information handling for the users to navigate.
- *Artifact*. It describes an abstract object to be transferred between the Web application and a user or vice versa as a result of an event execution.
- *Service*. It describes an activity or an action that the web application has.
- *Event*. It describes the trigger of an activity or action that might be carried out to obtain a result or artifact.
- *Non functional*. It describes the quality features or constrains for the web application.
- *Pre and pos condition*. It describes the performance of an event execution where a precondition is a required object state before the event can be executed and a post condition is the required object state after the event execution.

3 The concepts and the evaluation methodology

The concepts are enhanced with aspects that make them more powerful to model a particular view. These concepts are also used as scales to evaluate modeling tools. The definition of an evaluation scale for each concept is a task that requires the analysis of different modeling tools.

Table 2. Concepts and evaluation scales for the organizational level of abstraction

Concept \ Scale	1	2	3	4	5
Actor	Actor	---	Role	Type	Responsibility
Resource	Resource	Type	Actor using it	---	Actor supplying it
Goal	Goal	Priority	Problem	Opportunity	Verification
Task	Task	Who requests	Who executes	Hierarchy	Associated Goal.
Activity	Activity	Tasks supported	Hierarchy	How is activated	When is concluded
Business rule	Business rule	Associated concept	Origin	Type	Hierarchy
Quality	Quality	Associated concept	---	Origin	Measure

Table 3. Aspects and evaluation scales for the conceptual level of abstraction

Concept \ Scale	1	2	3	4	5
Actor	Actor	---	Role	Type	Responsibility
Artifact	Artifact	Actor or function supplying	---	Actor or function requiring	Artifact state
Goal	Goal	Who establish it, Associated to a function	Assigned priority	Measure, Failure cause	Opportunity to solve a problem
Function	Function	Who starts it	Who uses it	Hierarchy	The product
Event	Event	Who fires it, What is the start state,	What is produced, Hierarchy	Who receives the product, Owner function	Final state
Constraint	Constraint	Type	Who defines it	To who or what applies	Who or what enforces it
Non functional requirement	Constraint	Who proposes it To what is applied.	Type of requirement.	Measure to verify compliance.	What happens if not fulfilled.

Table 4. Concepts and evaluation scales for the web level of abstraction

Scale / Concept	1	2	3	4	5
Navigation page - Relationship	Navigation page	Nav. page - Relationship	User Profile	Navigation help	Access constraints
User profile (Role)	User profile	Role	Role changes allowed	Services per user	Business process state
Class (object)	Class (objct)	Attributes	Relationships	Methods	Tye of relationships
Artifact	Artifact	---	Type	Supplier	User
Goal	Who defines it	Associated service,	Priority	Measure	Failure cause, Opportunity to solve it
Service	Related events	Hierarchy, Requesting User	Executing agent, Result.	Result final user	Owner page
Event	Event	Service owner, Hierarchy,	Implementing class	Who requests	Shared or not
Pre and post condition	Post condition	Pre condition	---	---	Associated event
Non functional requirement	Non functional requirement	Who proposes it, To what is applied.	Type of requirement.	Measure to verify compliance	What happens if not fulfilled.

The scale is defined for each concept using the capabilities related to the concept. Also, a desired capability mentioned in the literature may be used in the definition of a scale. Following a well-known approach from the economics and management disciplines [10], to each concept a scale between 0 and 5 is assigned which is going to be used to evaluate one of the modeling capabilities. The order assigned to the scales is intuitive and relatively arbitrary; however, it can be changed easily. The concepts evaluation scales facilitate the comparison of different modeling tools capabilities (see table 2, 3 and 4). The evaluation scale is obtained by first taking a list of the capabilities of one tool, and then a list of capabilities from a second tool, from a third, until all selected tools are analyzed.

The evaluators have to evaluate the three levels of abstraction for all concepts. For each modeling tool and for each aspect a_i, a corresponding evaluation e_i is obtained. The results are displayed in a table for easy of comparison and a total score is obtained for each tool and for each level of abstraction as Σe_i. A tool that scores better than other it possibly has more capabilities to model requirements at the corresponding level of abstraction than the other. The methodology assigns a value to each concept of the method. For example, the precondition and post condition concept at the web level of abstraction; if the method has the post condition aspect, it will have 1 point. If the method has also the precondition aspect, it will have 2 points. If the method has the post condition, precondition and the associated event aspect, it will have 5 points.

4   Evaluation results

To evaluate the scale the following tools were evaluated (tables 5, 6, 7a and 7b): i*, Tropos, EKD, BPM-UML, NDT, OO-Method/OOWS, and OOWS [5, 7, 4, 8, 9, 10, 11, 12, 16]. At organizational level, BPM-UML obtains good scores for this level of abstraction, and i* has the lowest score.

Table 5. Organizational level evaluation of the tools

Organizational level	Max. Value	I*	Tropos	EKD	BPM-UML
Actor	5	5	5	5	5
Resource	5	5	5	2	5
Goal	5	1	3	4	3
Task	5	2	4	3	2
Activity	5	0	2	0	4
Business rule	5	2	0	5	4
Quality	5	3	4	4	4
Total	**35**	18	23	23	27

Table 6. Organizational level evaluation of the tools

Conceptual level	Max. Value	I*	Tropos	NDT	EK D	BPM-UML	OO-Method
Actor	5	5	5	5	5	5	1
Artifact	5	5	5	1	4	5	4
Goal	5	1	3	2	4	3	1
Function	5	2	2	4	5	5	2
Event	5	0	1	2	0	4	3
Constrain	5	2	0	4	5	4	5
No functional	5	3	4	3	4	4	0
Total	**35**	17	20	21	27	30	16

Table 7(a). Web level evaluation of the tools (business process)

Web level	Max. Value	Tropos	OO-Method / OOWS	NDT	OOWS
User profile	5	3	4	3	4
Class	5	0	5	5	5
Artifact	5	4	4	1	4
Service	5	3	3	4	3
Event	5	1	3	2	2
Pre and post condition	5	2	5	4	3
No functional	5	3	0	3	0
Total	**35**	16	24	22	21

Table 8(a). Web level evaluation of the tools (pure navigation)

Web level	Max. Value	Tropos	OO-Method / OOWS	NDT	OOWS
Navegational page – relationship	5	1	5	5	5
User profile	5	3	4	3	4
Goal	5	3	0	2	0
Artifact	5	4	4	1	4
Service	5	3	3	4	3
Total	25	14	16	15	16

The tools were evaluated with respect to the parameters defined for the approach presented here. During the evaluation of tools, their own characteristics are shown, for example, the quality aspects of a business process are modeled as qualitative goals using BPM-UML. At conceptual level, the result shows the capacities of each tool, for example, EKD obtains good scores for this level, but OO-Method has the lowest score. At web level, the result shows the capacities of each tool, for example, OO-Method/OOWS obtains good scores for this level, but Tropos has the lowest score.

5 Evaluation methodology of products

Concepts allow to evaluate the products of different tools when they are applied to a specific problem. To show the use, a case study was applied to the i*, Tropos, EKD and BPM-UML tools. The products of these tools were evaluated with the methodology of products. The evaluation capability can be completed with the product evaluation. A brief example of the product methodology is presented. The variables defined for the analysis and evaluation of the products are the following: a) workflow, b) order execution in the function, c) tree of decomposition, d) organization, and e) clear identification of the elements. To each variable a value 0 or 5 is assigned, 5 if the tool has the variable or 0 if it has not the variable. The values assigned to the variables are relatively arbitrary; however, it can be changed. The results in the product evaluation of the tools are presented in the table 8. This evaluation shows that BPM-UML has good score, but in the product evaluation EKD has the best score. The product is an additional reference to select a modeling tool (capability – product).

Table 8. Product evaluation

	Work flow	Order execution	Tree of decomposition	Organization	Identification of elements	Total
I*	5	0	5	0	0	10
Tropos	5	0	5	0	5	15
EKD	5	5	5	5	5	25
BPM	5	0	5	5	5	20

Conclusion

There are many proposals to model requirements and each one has its own elements. Some use the same concepts but the names are different, which makes it complex and laborious to compare the tools. The approach presented here unifies the various terminologies, increases the knowledge about modeling concepts, and proposes an evaluation approach for the tools modeling capabilities and techniques. This helps to select the tool that is more appropriate to the needs of a problem domain. Additionally, the approach evaluates the products when different tools are applied to a definition problem. A set of variables is proposed to evaluate the complexity of each model. This helps to know how many capacities the tools has, and also how complex the models are when a specific tool is used. A future work is use metrics on the products or models when different tools are applied. The approach has been used to evaluate e-learning systems [16]. Additionally, it has been applied in the development of various study cases to evaluate virtual reality tools and to clearly appreciate the concepts that the tools allow to model.

References

1. James Pasley, "How BPEKL and SOA are changing web services development", IEEE Internet Computing. May – June 2005.
2. Peter F. Green, Michael Rosemann y Marta Indulska, "Ontological Evaluation of Enterprisee systems Interoperability Using ebXML", IEEE Transactions on Knowledge and Data Engineering, Vol 17, No. 5, IEEE Computer Society, may 2005.
3. Mersevy T. and Fenstermacher K., "Transforming software development: and MDA road map", IEEE Computer Society, September 2005.
4. H. E. Eriksson and M. Penker, Bussiness, Modeling with UML, Chichester, UK, Wiley Editorial, 2000.
5. E. Yu, Modelling Strategic Relation for Process Reengineering, Universidad de Toronto, Canada, 1995. Thesis submitted for the degree of Doctor of Philosophy.
6. A. Ginige and S. M. "Web Engineering: An Introduction" IEEE Multimedia, pp 1-5, Jan-Mar 2001.
7. Peter F. Green, Michael Rosemann y Marta Indulska, "Ontological Evaluation of Enterprisee systems Interoperability Using ebXML", IEEE Transactions on Knowledge and Data Engineering, Vol 17, No. 5, IEEE Computer Society, may 2005.
8. Olsina, Luis A., Metodología cuantitativa para la evaluación y comparación de la calidad de sitios web. Tesis doctoral. Fac. de Ciencias Exactas, Univ. Nacional de La Plata, noviembre de 1999.
9. Devanshu Dhyani, Wee Keong Ng, and Sourav S. Bhowmick, A survey of web metrics, ACM computer survey, Vol 34, No. 4. December 2002, pp. 469-503.
10. Bubenko J., Brash D. y Stirna J. EKD User Guide, Royal Institute of technology (KTH) and Stockholm University, Stockholm, Sweden, Dept. of Computer and Systems Sciences, 1998.
11. M. J. Escalona, J. torres, M. Mejías, A. M. Reina. From the requirement to the conceptual model in NDT. III Taller de Ingeniería del Software Orientado a la Web Alicante, Spain. November, 2003
12. E. Insfrán, O.Pastor y R. Wieringa, "Requirements Engineering-Based conceptual Modelling", Requirements Engineering Springer-Verlang, vol. 2, pp. 7:61-72, 2002.
13. J. Gómez, C. Cachero and O. Pastor, "Conceptual modeling of device-independent Web applications" IEEE Multimedia, vol. 8 issue: 2 , pp 26-39, April-June 2001.
14. L. Liu, E. Yu Intentional Modeling to support Identity Management 23rd Int. Conference on Conceptual Modeling (ER 2004). Shanghai, China, November, 2004. Springer. pp. 555-566.
15. J. Fons, O. Pastor, P. Valderas y M. Ruiz, OOWS: Un método de producción de software en ambientes web. 2005. http://oomethod.dsic.upv.es/anonimo/..%5Cfiles%5CBookChapter%5Cfons02b.pdf
16. Eduardo Islas P., Eric Zabre B. y Miguel Pérez R., "Evaluación de herramientas de software y hardware para el desarrollo de aplicaciones de realidad virtual", consultado en el 2005, http://www.iie.org.mx/boletin022004/tenden2.pdf

Integration Ontology for Distributed Database

Ana Muñoz[1], Jose Aguilar[2], and Rodrigo Martinez[3]

1 Instituto Universitario Tecnológico de Ejido. Mérida Venezuela
anamunoz@ula.ve,
2 Uiversidad de Los Andes. CEMISID. Mérida Venezeula.
aguilar@ula.ve
3 Uiversidad de Murcia. Murcia España.
rodrigo@um.es

Abstract. In this work we will study the problem of the design of the "Integration Model for Distributed Database System". We particularly design the canonical model through the ontological handling of the information. The ontology is designed in a way that allows the description of a database like a set of representative terms of its different components. In this ontology, the definitions use classes, relations, functions, among other things, of databases, to describe their components, operations and restrictions, as well as, the process of integration. These databases can be Relational, Fuzzy, Intelligent and Multimedia.

1 Introduction

The interoperability between different systems information is one of the most critical aspects in the daily operation of many organizations. In the last decade this preoccupation was increased with the proliferation of different databases, with different data models, that run in different platforms. The systems of distributed databases, also known as federated databases, allow to have available the information from different sources of intelligence that can be heterogeneous, distributed and independent. A federated database acts like a front-end application of manifold component. The federated database provides operations for the access to each component, maintaining the consistency of information between the diverse sources and providing a uniform access method to the services that each component offers.

The diversity of programming languages, data models and methods of integration, determine different styles in the architecture for a federated database, that varies from a loosely coupled to tightly coupled approach. In general, the tightly coupled systems integrate the diverse sources of intelligence through a global conceptual scheme, normally denominated canonical model, providing a uniform vision of the diverse components at a high level. The use of a canonical model hides the structural differences between the different components and gives to the user the illusion to be accessing a simple centralized database. On the other hand, on the

Please use the following format when citing this chapter:

Muñoz, A., Aguilar, J., Martinez, R., 2006, in IFIP International Federation for Information Processing, Volume 219, Advanced Software Engineering: Expanding the Frontiers of Software Technology, eds. Ochoa, S., Roman, G.-C., (Boston: Springer), pp. 85–93.

systems tightly coupled the integration of the components is based on a language of common access that all the components must decide, in a way that all the functions are standardized. In this work we will deal with the design of the "Canonical Model for Integration of Distributed Databases". Particularly, we set out to design the canonical model through the ontological handling of the information. This ontology allows describing a database like a set of terms that represent its different components. In this ontology, the definitions use classes, relations, functions, among other things, of the databases, to describe its components, restrictions, operations, etc. The reason of using ontologies is that they define concepts and relations within a taxonomic frame, whose conceptualization is represented, of a formal way, legible and usable. Of this form, ontology is a common and shared understanding of a domain that can be used to communicate heterogeneous systems [7].

The integration of tightly coupled federated database has been treated in previous works for relational and objects databases. Alvarez in its work presents a proposal of binary integration for the generation of a federation of component databases [1]. In addition, it presents a scheme to use the local components through a query language. In the work of Abello et al., they present an integration model in real time to databases using the canonical model BLOOM [2]. These works use the architecture for federated databases of Shet&Larson [10]. In previous works [8] we have represented an architecture for the integration of database where it is necessary a canonical model.

Like continuation of that work, in this article the ontological taxonomies that compose the databases integration architecture are described, and the Canonical Model is designed using this ontological notion. This way, the processes of integration of the different types of databases and of resolution of conflicts are defined through the ontology. In addition, the integration ontology is translated to first-order logic predicate, so that from it we design the mechanisms of consultation, update and data mining for Intelligent Distributed Database. This article shows in one first part, the theoretical aspect on which the same one is based, which includes to the distributed databases, as well as the ontology concepts. In the second part the integration process is described through ontological schemes, as well as its axioms that defines the logic expressions of the integration process. The ontological schemes of the component databases are described in other work [11]. Thus, the fundamental aspect of this work is to propose a ontological frame based on sentences of First-Order Logical Predicate (LPO) for the integration of a federation of databases.

2   Theoretical Aspects

2.1   Distributed Databases

The distributed databases talk about the integration of necessities of no local storage and processing where is necessary to interchange originating information of different sites [1, 2]. The systems of distributed databases integrate systems of diverse databases, to give to the users a global vision of the information available. The decentralization of the information promotes the heterogeneity in its handling. This can occurs in many levels, from the form and meaning of each data to the format and the storage media that are chosen to keep it. From the functional organization, the systems of distributed database are divided in two classes: A homogenous distributed database that is a collection of multiple data. The homogenous systems are looked like a centralized system, but instead of storing to all the data in a single place the data are distributed in several sites communicated by the network. The heterogeneous systems are characterized to handle different database in each node. An important subclass is the Federated Databases, which integrate information from heterogeneous databases, and present a global access to the users, with transparent methods to use the total information in the system. The main characteristic is the autonomy that the local databases, also called Component Databases, conserve. In order to build the federation of Component Databases, it is necessary to provide a mechanism that is able to obtain a global scheme of databases, which allows a transparent access to the different databases existing [10]. The heterogeneity in the component databases can be presented in several aspects: hardware, software, data modeling, and semantic aspect, among others. A System of Federated Database (SFDB) is classified like weakly connected or strongly connected, based on the idea of whom handles the federation and how their components are integrated. A SFDB is weakly connected if the responsibility to create and to maintain the federation falls to the user, and there is not control on the part of the federated system and its administrations. A federation is strongly connected when the federation and its administrators are responsible for the creation and the maintenance of the same one, and participate actively in the control of the Component Database. A strongly federated system connection can be of two types: With unique federation, if it allows the creation and management of an only federated scheme. With multiple federations, if it allows the creation and management of multiple federated schemes. Each SFDB has an architecture of schemes to surpass the syntactic and semantic heterogeneities. Shet&Larson [10] proposes an architecture of schemes for a SFDB composed by: i) *Local Scheme*. It is the conceptual scheme of the Systems of Component Database that integrates the Federation; ii) *Component Scheme*. The conceptual schemes of the component databases are translate to a canonical model, that is a common data modeling for all the databases that are going to compose the federation; iii) *Scheme of Export*. In this scheme is described the part of the component schemes that are going to be shared as well as their location and access control; iv) *Federated Scheme*, in this scheme is made the integration of the multiple schemes of exportation; v) *External Scheme*. This is the scheme for each user and/or application of the SFDB.

2.2 Canonical Model

The ability of representation of the database comes given by its data modeling. A data modeling is made up of structures, operations and the restrictions in the use of them. The ability of representation of a data modeling is made up of two factors[9]: i) *Expressivity*. The expressivity of a data modeling is the degrees in which a model can directly represent the concepts that it conform. ii) *Semantic Relativism*. The semantic relativism of data modeling is the power of its operations to derive external schemes.

When different databases form a federation, they require a integration data modeling, called Canonical Data Model (CDM). The CDM is the element that processes the query and updates that are made to the federation. Thus, following the architecture of five levels of Shet&Larson [10], we can develop a common CDM to all the federation. The use of a CDM solves the problem of syntactic heterogeneity, consequence of the use of different native data models. The heterogeneity semantic, resulting of different conceptualizations from Component databases, is solved in the process of integration of schemes. The CDM has the following characteristics: i) Generalization: it is the process by means of which, from two or more entities is constructed a new entity; ii) Association: it defines a new entity from the relations between two or more entities; iii) Classification: allows to group entities in classes, that is constructs a new entity from the common characteristics of other entities. The CDM must support the definition of new operations and restrictions, must allow the implementation of integration operators, among other things [9]. We will use ontologies to represent our CDM, since they allow integrating databases using intelligence during the process of conformation of the federation, as well as the semantic enrichment through the integration of the databases with its concepts, operations and restrictions.

2.3 Ontology

A definition of Ontology in terms of database is the following [4, 7]: "***Ontology is a database that describes the concepts of the world of some domain, some of its properties and how these concepts are related between them*** ". The knowledge represented within ontology is formalized through five components: i) *Concepts or classes*: They are the ideas to be formalized. They belong to a certain domain of application, and can be organized in taxonomies; ii) *Relations*: They represent the interactions between the classes and are defined as a subgroup of a Cartesian product; iii) *Functions*: They are a special case of relations, where elements are generated by means of the calculation of a function; iv) *Instance*: they are used to represent elements or individuals in an ontology; v) *Axioms*: They serve to model sentences that always are going to be certain. They are used to represent knowledge and are used to represent the properties that concepts and instances must satisfy. For example: If animal class animal is mammalian; the instance dog is mammalian.

Classifications of ontologies have been done in agreement with the type of concept to describe and its use [4, 5]: i) *Terminological*: they specify the terms that are used to represent knowledge. Usually they are used to unify vocabulary in a certain domain; ii) *Knowledge Modeling*: they specify concepts related to the knowledge. They contain a rich internal structure and usually are fixed to the particular use of the knowledge that they describe; iii) *Ontologies of domain*: These ontologies are specific for a domain in concrete; iv) *Ontologies of tasks*: These ontologies represent the tasks that are susceptible to make in a domain in concrete; v) *General Ontologies*: They represent general information and nonspecific of a domain.

3   Design of an Intelligent Model of Integration for Federated Databases

The design of our CDM will be based an Ontologies. These ontologies describe to each one of the databases to integrate, as well as the integration process. In the following figure is shown our Intelligent Canonical Model (modeled in a Knowledge and Facts Database), and that has learning and reasoning mechanisms to carry out the integration process.

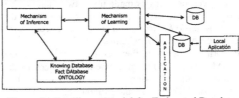

Figure 2. Intelligent Model for Federated Databases

The Federated Databases integrate information from local heterogeneous databases and allow the global access to the users. The main characteristic is the autonomy that the local databases or Component Databases conserve. In order to allow on a federation of Component Database, we need to provide an integration mechanism for obtaining a global approach of the resources of information of an organization. This is obtained through the canonical model.

3.1 Concepts of Federated Databases

A Federated Database is a component database that has operations and restrictions of integration. The Component Databases are the databases that conform the federation. In our case, these component databases can be: Object-oriented Databases, Relational Databases, Multimedia Databases, Fuzzy Databases, or Intelligent Databases; also a component database can be another federated Database. Each one of these component databases has their concepts, operations and restrictions. In figure 3 is shown the ontological scheme that describes the concepts of the federated databases.

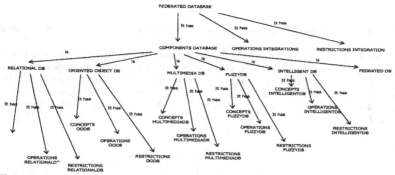

Figure 3. Ontological scheme of the components that integrate an Intelligent Distributed Database

In table 1 is described the ontological scheme of the figure 3 through axioms. These are used to define the ontology like logic expressions. Each axiom includes its description in natural language, and its logical expression.

Table 1. Axioms for the concepts of the Federated Databases

Sentence	LPO
A Federated database has component databases, and operations and restrictions of integration	∀ x FederatedDB(x) => Has (x,ComponentDB) ∧ Has (x,IntegrationOperation) ∧ Has (x,IntegrationRestriction)
The component databases can be relational databases, object-oriented databases, multimedia databases, fuzzy databases, intelligent databases and federated data bases	∀ x ComponentDB(x) => Is(x,RelationalDB) V Is (x, OODB) V Is (x, MultimediaDB) V Is (x, FuzzyDB) V Is (x, IntelligentDB) V Is (x, FedratedDB)
The Relational database has Concepts, Operations, and Restrictions	∀ x RelationalDB(x) => Has(x,ConceptsR) ∧ Has(x, OperationsR) ∧ Has(x, RestrictionsR)
The OODB has Concepts, Operations, and Restrictions	∀ x OODB(x) => Has(x,ConceptsOO) ∧ Has(x, OperationsOO) ∧ Has(x, RestrictionsOO)
The Multimedia Database has Concepts, Operations, and Restrictions	∀ x MultimediaDB(x) => Has(x,ConceptsMM) ∧ Has(x, OperatinsMM) ∧ Has(x, RestrictionsMM)
The fuzzy database has Concepts, Operations, and Restrictions	∀ x FuzzyDB(x) => Has(x,ConceptsFuzzy) ∧ Has(x, OperationsFuzzy) ∧ Has(x, RestrictionsFuzzy)
The Intelligent Database Concepts, Operations, and Restrictions	∀ x IntelligentsDB(x) => Has(x,ConceptsInt) ∧ Has(x, OperationsInt) ∧ Has(x, RestrictionsInt)

3.2 Operations of Integration in a Database Federation

We will use the operations of integration according to Batini and Lenzerini [3, 6], which is made in phases. Next the characteristics of these phases are described.

Preintegration. In this phase is defined the order of integration of the databases and the parts of the databases to integrate. The integration order can be binary when two schemes are integrated simultaneously, and n-Aryan when they integrate n schemes simultaneously. Also, the policies of integration as far as the access restrictions and priority in the access to Component databases are defined. This procedure is the same when we form a new federation or when we can incorporate a component database to an existing Database Federation.

Comparison of the schemes. The databases are compared and analyzed to determine the correspondence between concepts and to detect the possible conflicts. Once the conflicts are detected, they are sent to the Conflicts Management System to solve them through a system of rules.

Union and Reconstruction. Once solved the conflicts, the union of the different schemes from the component databases is made. The goal of this activity is to conform or to align schemes to make them compatible for its integration. It has operations like: transform an atomic concept into another one, eliminate redundant relations, create hierarchy of generalization.

In figure 4 is shown the ontological scheme that describes the operations of integration of a Database Federation.

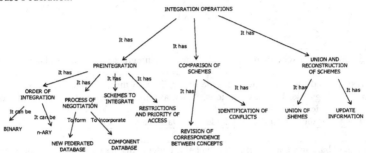

Figure 4. Ontological Scheme to Operations of Integration for a Database Federation

The Axioms for the operations of integration of a Database Federation are in the table 2:

Table 2. Axioms for the operations of a Database Federation

Sentence	LPO
The operation of integration has the phase of preintegration, comparison of schemes and conformation of the canonical model	$\forall$ x OperatiónIntegration(x) => Has (x,Preintegration) $\wedge$ Has(x,ComparisonSchemes) $\wedge$ Has (x,ConformationCM)
The Preintegration defines the integration order, the negotiation process, the schemes to integrate, the restrictions and the priority of access	$\forall$ Preintegration(x) =>Has(x, OrderIntegration) $\wedge$ Has(x,ProcessNegotiation) $\wedge$ Has(x,SchemestoIntegrate) $\wedge$ Has(x, RestrictionsofAccess) $\wedge$ Has(x, PriorityofAccess)
The Order of integration of the databases can be binary or n-Aryan	$\forall$ x OrderIntegration(x) => Is(x,BinaryIntegration) V Is(x, n-aryanIntegartion)
In the Process of negotiation a new federation is formed or a component database is added to an existing Database Federation	$\forall$ x ProcessNegotiation(x) => Formed(x,NewFederatedDB) V Added(x, ComponentDB)
In the comparison of schemes must be reviewed the correspondence between concepts to determine the conflicts	$\forall$ x SchemesComparison(x) => Has (x,ReviewCorrespondencebetweenConcepts) $\wedge$ Has(x,IdentificationofConflictsIntegartions)
A binary order of integration integrates two schemes simultaneously	$\forall$ x BinaryIntegration(x) => Integrate(x,TwoSchemes)
The integration order n-Aryan is the one that Integrate n schemes simultaneously	V x N-AryanIntegration(x) => Integrate(x,NSchemes)
The access restrictions are the authorizations to accede to the component databases that conformed the federation	$\forall$ x RestrictionsAccess(x) => ItAuthorizes (x,AccessComponentDB)
The access priority establishes the order of access to the component databases	$\forall$ x AccessPriority(x) => Establishes(x,OrderofAccesstoComponentDB)

The union and reconstruction of schemes define the union of schemes and the update of the information in the model	∀ x UnionandReconstructionSchemes(x) => Have(x,UnionSchemes) ∧ Have(x,UpdateofInformation)

3.3 Restrictions of Integration in a Database Federation

In the integration of the databases, the following types of conflicts can appear:

- Conflicts in Tables: Conflicts in the Name of tables, Conflicts in the Structure of the tables, objects and multimedia elements, Conflicts in the Restrictions of Integrity.
- Conflicts of Attributes: Conflicts in name of Attributes, Conflicts in Values by Default, Conflicts by Restrictions of the Attributes Values, Conflicts by the Cardinality and degree of Atomicity, Conflicts in the Representation of the Information.
- Conflicts of Data: Conflicts between the values, when equivalent instances have different values because the collected data are incorrect or are obsolete. Differences in the representation.
- Conflicts in Rules: Simultaneous firing of Rules, Contradiction between rules.

In figure 5 is shown the ontological scheme that describes the conflicts.

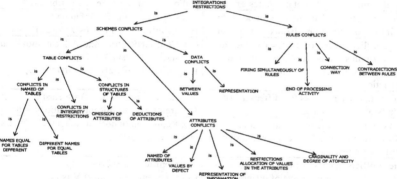

Figure 5. Ontological scheme of the Integration Restrictions for a Database Federation.

The Axioms of the restrictions of integration for a Database Federation are in table 3:

Table 3. Axioms for the restrictions in a Database Federation

Sentence	LPO
The integration restrictions can be conflicts in schemes or conflicts in rules	∀ x Integrationrestrictions (x) => Is(x,ConflictsSchemes) V Is(x,ConflictsRules)
The conflicts in scheme can be conflicts in tables or conflicts in attributes or conflicts in data	∀ x ConflictsSchemes(x) => Is(x,ConflictsTable) V Is(x,ConflictsAttributes) V Is (x,ConflictsData)
The conflicts in tables can be in name of tables, structure of table, of object or of multimedia element or in integrity restrictions	∀ x ConflictsTable(x) => Is (x,ConflictsNamedTable) V Is (x, ConflictsStructureTable) V Is (x,ConflictsStructureObject) V Is(x, ConflictStructureMM) V Is (x,ConflictRestrictionIntegrity)
The tables name conflicts arises when different names for equal tables or equal names for different tables exist	∀ x ConflictsNamedTable (x) => DifferentNamedTables(x,EqualTables) V EqualNamedTables(x,DiferentsTables)
The conflict in table structure happens when there are attributes that are omitted or when there are attributes that are deduced	∀ x ConflictsStructureTable (x) => Is(x, AttributesOmitted) V Is(x,AttributesDeduced)

The conflict in structure of Object happens when there are attributes of the object that are omitted or when there are attributes of the object that are deduced	$\forall$ x ConflictsStructureObject(x) => Is(x,AttributesObOmitted) V Is(x,AtributtesObDeduced)
The conflict in multimedia structure happens when there are attributes MM omitted or when there are attributes MM that are deduced	$\forall$-x ConflictStructureMM => Is(x,AttributesMMOmited) V Is(x,AttributesMMDeduced)
The conflicts in attributes can be conflicts in name attribute or conflicts in values by default or conflicts of restrictions of values of the attributes or conflicts of cardinality or conflicts in the representation of the information	$\forall$ x ConflictsAttributes(x) => Is(x,ConflictoNombreAtributo) V Is (x,ConflictsValuesByDefault) V Is (x,ConflictsRestrictionofAlocationsofValues) V Is (x,ConflictsCardinality) V Is (x,ConflictosRepresentactóonInformation)
The conflicts in name of Attributes has different names for equivalent attributes or equal names for different attributes exist	$\forall$ x ConflictsNomedAttributes(x) => HasDifferentNames(x,EquivalentAttributes) V HsEqualNames(x,DiferentAttributes)
The conflicts in values by default occur by definition of the values deduced by default	$\forall$ x ConflictsValueByDefault(x) => Has(x,DefinitionOfValuesDeduced)
The conflicts by Restrictions of Values to the Attributes can be conflicts in the data types and conflicts in the domain of restrictions.	$\forall$ x ConflictsRestrictionofAllocationofValues(x) => Is(x,ConflictsinDataType) V Is(x,ConflictsinRestrictionsofDomain)
A cardinality conflict is the difference of details of the attributes	$\forall$ xCardinalityConflict(x) => Has(x, DifferentLevel fromRepresentationofAttributes)
The Conflicts in the representation of information are the different domain that an attribute represents	$\forall$ x RepresentationofInformacionConflict(x) => Has(x,DifferentDomain)
The conflicts in data can be conflicts between values or conflicts of differences in the representation	$\forall$ x ConflictsData(x) => Is (x, ConflictsbetweenValues) V Is (x, ConflictsofDifferencesintheRepresentation)
A conflict between values arises when equal instances have different values	$\forall$ x ConflictsbetweenValues(x) => Has(x,EqualInstancesofData) $\wedge$ Has(x, DifferentValuesofData)
The representation differences has different representations for a same data	$\forall$ x ConflictofDiferencesofRepresentation(x) => Has(x,DifferentRepresentationOfDifferentData)
A conflict in rule can be a firing simultaneously of rules, or can be a conflict in the connection way or can be conflict in the aim of the processing of rules, or can be a contradiction between rules	$\forall$ x ConflictinRule(x) => Is (x, FiringSimultaneouslyofRules) V Is (x, ConflictintheConnectionWay) V Is (x,EndOfProcessing) V Is (x,ContradictionBetweenRules)
A simultaneous firing of rules is when an event activates more than one rule	$\forall$ x SimultaneousFiringofRules (x) => Isa(x, ShootsmorethanoneRule)

4 Conclusions

In this work the ontological schemes that represent the process of integration of databases are presented, based on the architecture of Shet&Larson [10] for federated databases. The development of the ontologies is used like scheme that allows making the intelligent integration of a federation of databases. Particularly, the canonical model must have the ability of representation of the different data models from level of its structures, operations and restrictions of the databases which conform the federation, solving the heterogeneity problems that can be presented. We use ontology like representation of the canonical model, since it allows taxonomically to describe the concepts in the domain of the databases and its properties. In addition, with the ontology we will be able to design management systems based on mechanisms of reasoning and learning. Thus, our Model of Intelligent Integration of Federated databases is intelligent and extensibility. In our representation of the Model of Intelligent Integration of Federated Databases we found the taxonomies that describe the concepts, operations and restrictions of the process of integration of the databases. The axioms interpret the taxonomy and will allow translating the ontologies to a language of knowledge. With them, new knowledge could be obtained and extracted.

In the future, a language of manipulation of the Intelligent Distributed Database will be designed using our ontology. For this, an inference mechanism must be designed that allow to reason during the processes of query and update over the Distributed Database. In addition, a mechanism of manipulation of the Canonical Model must be designed (learning) to update the knowledge. Also, from the inference mechanism tasks of data mining will be able to be done, such as generate patterns of access of users of the system to create virtual communities, extract new knowledge derived from the integration of the databases, etc.

References

1. Alvarez Carrión, G.; "Integración de esquemas en bases de datos heterogéneas fuertemente acopladas". Master thesis, Universidad de las Américas, Puebla. México 1999
2. Abello A., M. Oliva, J. Samos, and F. Saltor; "Information System Architecture for secure Data Warehousing". In Proc. of the 3rd Int. Workshop on Engineering Federated Information Systems (EFIS), pag. 33-40. 2000
3. Batini C., Lenzerini M.; "A comparative analysis of methodologies for database schema integration", ACM Computing Surveys 17, 4, December 1976.
4. Bertino E., Catania B., Zarri Gian P.; "Intelligent Database System", Addison-Wesley. 2001. http://ksi.cpsc.ucalgary.ca/KAW/KAW97/blazquez/
5. Corcho O., Fernandez-López M., Gomez-Perez A., "Methodologies, tools and languages for building ontologies. Where is their meeting point? Data & Knowledge Engineering 46 (2003) 41-64. Elsevier.
6. Fernandez-Breis J., Martinez-Béjar R.; "A cooperative framework for integrating ontologies"; Elsiever Science Human Computer Studies 2002.
7. Gruber, T. R. "A Translation Approach to Portable Ontology Specifications. KSL Report", 1993, http://ksl-web.stanford.edu/abstracts_by_author/Gruber,T..papers.html
8. Muñoz A., Aguilar J.; "Architecture for Distributed Intelligent Databases". IEEE, 13th Euromicro Conference on Parallel, Distributed and Network-based Processing, Euromicro-PDP 2005, pp 322-327
9. Saltor F., Castellanos M, García-Solaco M; "Suitability of data models as canonical models for federated databases"; Universitat Politècnica de Catalunya.
10. Shet P, Larson J., "Federated Database System for managing distributed, heterogeneous and autonomous databases". ACM Computing Surveys 22, 1990 pp 173, 236

SSP: A Simple Software Process for Small-Size Software Development Projects

Sergio F. Ochoa[1], José A. Pino[1], Luis A. Guerrero[1], César A. Collazos[2]

[1] Department of Computer Science
Universidad de Chile
Blanco Encalada 2120, Santiago, Chile
{sochoa, jpino, luguerre}@dcc.uchile.cl

[2] FIET, System Department
University of Cauca
Popayán, Sector Tulcán, Colombia
ccollazo@unicauca.edu.co

Abstract. A large number of software development projects in Latin-American countries are small-size, poorly defined and time pressured. These projects usually involve under qualified people. Provided that well-known software development models have shown limited applicability in such scenario, developers usually carry out ad-hoc software processes. Therefore, the obtained results are unpredictable. This article presents a Simple Software Process (SSP) for small-size software projects involving under qualified people. The proposal is motivated by current practice in Chile. SSP proposes a step-by-step process which structures the development activities and it improves the process visibility for clients and team members. Furthermore, SSP formally includes "the user/client" as an active role to be played during the project. This process has been used in 22 software projects and the results are encouraging.

1. Introduction

Most software development projects in Chile are information systems of small or medium size (1-2 months or 3-6 months) [17]. Typically, these projects involve time pressured activities and clients reacting just when they detect the need for a software solution [9, 21]. For that reason, these projects have a high rate of volatile requirements [17].

Typically, qualified developers are involved in large or medium-size projects whereas small software projects are carried out by under-qualified or inexperienced

Please use the following format when citing this chapter:

Ochoa, S.F., Pino, J.A., Guerrero, L.A., Collazos, C.A., 2006, in IFIP International Federation for Information Processing, Volume 219, Advanced Software Engineering: Expanding the Frontiers of Software Technology, eds. Ochoa, S., Roman, G.-C., (Boston: Springer), pp. 94–107.

software developers [17, 21]. The reactionary development scenario and the lack of clear guidelines to face the process, push developers to follow an ad-hoc development process. A recent study carried out by Sacre concludes that software processes in Chile tend to be chaotic and unpredictable, because they do not have a guiding development model [17]. Besides, each development is influenced by variables like type of project, client and development team. It shows how immature are the processes in this scenario. As a consequence, software projects in this scenario cannot assure the development time and cost nor the quality of the final product [14, 17].

The heavyweight software methodologies are limited to support such scenario. This is because they involve several stages and roles that require an important amount of communication and coordination in order to get a final product. This required bureaucracy jeopardizes the applicability of such software models.

On the other hand, there are the lightweight or agile methodologies that could have an interesting applicability to the described scenario. However, the high clients/users availability required to support the development process makes these processes unsuitable. The need to develop in an asynchronous and distributed way is another important limitation to adopt lightweight software processes in this scenario.

Alternatively, in order to solve the stated problem, this paper presents a software process called Simple Software Process (SSP), which has been designed to guide small-size software development projects in immature scenarios. This methodology was slowly evolving, as experience with real word cases was accruing.

Next section presents the critical issues which give rise to most problems in the software projects. Section 3 presents the related work and analyzes the applicability of the best known software processes to immature scenarios. Section 4 presents the proposed software process. Section 5 analyzes the results obtained after applying the methodology. Finally, section 6 states the conclusions of this work and the future related activities.

2. Critical Issues

Based on the studies of the local software industry conducted by Sacre [17], Stein [21] and IDC [10] during 2002, and based on several reported experiences and authors' experiences, a set of critical issues has been identified. Some of these issues present facts, which may not be changed and thus, any proposed solution must cope with them. These issues are the following ones:

Deadlines Determined by Need. Typically, the project deadlines are determined by the need of the client for deploying the software solution in his/her organization. Typically the available time is shorter or equal than the required one to do a good job. Therefore, it should be assumed deadlines will be difficult to reach and work will be done under pressure.

Asynchronous and Distributed Work. Most team members usually work in a distributed and asynchronous setting with little time dedicated to the project. Each member has allocated a time quantum to carry out the work and he/she has little time for coordination and integration activities [21].

Under Qualified Developers. Typically, development teams are composed of a senior engineer acting as project manager, and a set of senior students of Computer Science and Technology or junior engineers with little expertise in software development and teamwork [17, 10]. Although technically they are able to tackle a problem, they have difficulties to work as team members, to interact with users/clients and to identify/manage requirement changes and to handle risk and unpredictable problems. Most of them have little time assigned to the project and they work in an asynchronous and distributed way. Each member of the team plays more than one role, e.g., project manager/tester or analyst/programmer, but the rights and duties associated to each role are not explicitly defined [21]. In such cases, the project manager assigns activities based on his own best judgment [9]. As an example, we can mention that it is possible to observe programmers making design decisions, or that some tasks are simply not carried out because the project manager forgot to assign them.

On the other hand, there are further critical issues that need to be managed. The inadequate management of these issues produces most problems appearing in this type of projects. The critical issues to be managed during small development projects in immature scenarios are the following ones:

Clients Availability. Usually, the client has little time to interact with the development team. Many tasks involving the client, such as information providing, decision-making, review of prototypes, are accomplished late because his/her lack of time [21].

Requirement Stability. Most of these software projects are consequences of clients' reaction triggered by the identification of a need for a software solution. Therefore, software projects are not well conceived and matured at start time with the requirements elicitation. It produces permanent changes of the requirements and a lack of visibility of the software project [17]. Clients feel they have the right to adjust the requirement without paying extra money because the developers are not realizing what they want. This is one of the main causes of conflicts between clients and developers.

Coordination Activities. Most team members are not full time dedicated to the project and they work in an asynchronous and distributed way. There are no clearly defined roles in the team and there are no clear rights and duties associated to each team member [21]. Project managers assign activities to team members based on their own best judgment [9]. In addition, they are in charge of coordinating these team members activities based on some ad-hoc strategy. In a development scenario with many low dedicated, distributed and beginner developers is too easy to lose control of the project.

Project Visibility. Typically there is not enough time to do a proper development, therefore management and control activities are superficially done. There is high unplanned parallelism related to the tasks of team members, which originates an unnecessary workload and conflicts of scope. Typically, it is difficult to determine the advance status of the project and the workload required to finish it. It generates conflicts with clients and within the development team [17, 9].

Effort Estimation. The project duration and the initial functionality are quite fixed; therefore the effort estimation is reduced to a money issue [14]. The time available to develop the project is directly related to the client's urgency to have the products. Sometimes such duration is not viable to get good products, but ignorance about the productivity of these work teams drives the company to take high-risk projects. Generally, these projects are finished late and/or the resulting products do not satisfy the client expectations [14].

Product delivery. It is often clear what the final product the project should deliver in terms of software code, but the same cannot be said for the corresponding documentation. The process is strongly focused on delivering software, but the documentation is either incomplete or totally forgotten. In addition, the contents of intermediate products (specification of requirements or document design) are not carefully studied to verify if they are appropriate for the applied development style. On the other hand, there are many development teams that produce only the requirements specification and the software of the final product. Generally, this lack of formal intermediate products is the main cause for communication and coordination problems within the work team [17]. Moreover, the informality to elicit, specify and use requirements in these projects is the most important cause for a conflictive climate both among developers themselves and between them and the client [21].

Although these critical issues are the source for several problems in this type of projects, there is a lack of guidelines to manage them. In addition, well-known web development models seem to be problematic to be used in contexts such as the Chilean one, because of they are so heavy weight as to be carried out in short time using novice developers. This situation forces software developers to use handmade procedures to develop the Web software products. Next section presents the related works and the strengths and weaknesses of several proposals that could be used to solve the problem.

3. Related Work

Most models reported in the literature for software development are oriented towards mature development scenarios. Some of them are known as heavyweight software models because of the bureaucracy required during their application to a project. On the other hand, there are lightweight or agile software processes that involve minimal bureaucracy, but high interaction among team members and between team members and the users/clients.

Heavyweight software processes seem to be problematic to be used in immature contexts, because they are so difficult to be carried out in a short time period by using developers. Some of the most representative heavyweight software processes include the following ones.

OOHDM (Object-Oriented Hypermedia Design Methodology). This is a development methodology for hypermedia applications, including Web applications [18, 20]. OOHDM offers a clearly defined process, which can be adopted using an incremental model or a prototype based model. It proposes five basic steps to carry out the development: *requisite elicitation, conceptual design, navigational design, abstract interface design* and *implementation*. Although the process is clear, it is not easy enough to be used by beginners in short time periods.

WSDM (Web Sites Design Method). This methodology uses a user-centered design strategy [4]. The design is driven by the views of different user-classes instead of being data-driven. This method is limited to "Kiosk Web Sites", i.e., Web applications that only display data, and can be navigated through themselves. WSDM is a variant of the waterfall model that involves four phases: *user modeling, conceptual design, implementation design* and *implementation*. One of the most important advantages of this model is the application of user requirements as a guide for the development process. As regards disadvantages, since the model is based on the waterfall model, WSDM is affected by its typical problems [2]. In addition, it is only focused on the design process and does not give a clear support for roles, asynchronous and distributed work and coordination activities.

WebComposition. This model describes a consistent approximation to the Web Applications development based on components [8]. Basically, this model follows a spiral process that involves three phases: *analysis and planning, design and implementation*. The process is simple and provides feedback about process and product in a continuous way. One limitation of this model is the disregard for user requirements as a guide for the development process. It is focused on the design of the product, and it forces to use WCML (WebComposition Markup Language) [7] to represent that design. In addition, this model supports a rapid development only if the work team has an available library of reusable components, which are appropriate to build the new product.

WebE (Web Engineering). WebE is a general model described by Pressman [16], which follows an evolving approach including six stages: *formulation, planning, analysis, engineering, Web Pages development, testing and user evaluation*. Although this model is well conceived, it is heavyweight to be carried out in a short time. Besides, it has some restrictions such as: it does not perform requirements management; it demands a great effort for product design; each phase requires specialists; and the roles of the work team are not clearly defined.

RUP (Rational Unified Process). RUP provides a disciplined approach to assigning tasks and responsibilities within a development organization [12]. Its goal is to ensure the production of high quality software that meets the needs of its end users within a predictable schedule and budget. This software process involves the following phases: *inception, elaboration, construction* and *transition*. Team members work toward the milestones that mark each phase completion by performing activities organized into nine disciplines.

These models were not designed to support small software projects carried out in immature scenarios. For that reason their complexity, formalism, lack of support for quick developments or lack of a formal participation of the client during the development process restrict their applicability. However, there are lightweight software processes or agile methods that can be used to overcome limitations of traditional software processes [6]. Some of the most known agile methods are the following ones:

Extreme Programming (XP). XP was created for small and medium size software projects where requirements are vague, change rapidly or are very critical [1]. XP was designed having in mind the problems with traditional programming methodologies with respect to deadlines and client satisfaction.

Scrum. Scrum was not conceived as an independent method, but a complement of other agile methods [19]. Scrum stresses management values and practices, and it does not include practices for the technical parts (requirements, design, implementation). For that reason, Scrum can be used in conjunction with another agile method. Scrum is a management and control process that implements process control techniques.

Crystal. Crystal is a family of methodologies created by Cockburn [3]. They are based on the fact that, comparing software construction with an engineering process makes us think about software "specifications" and "models", about its completeness, correctness and operation. The most exhaustively documented Crystal methodology is Crystal Clear (CC). CC can be used in small projects with medium criticality, although it can also be applied to critical projects if it is properly extended.

Feature Driven Development (FDD). FDD is an agile, iterative and adaptive method that it does not cover the complete software life cycle, but only the design and implementation phases. It is considered adequate for major mission critical projects [15]. FDD applies an iterative development with the best found practices to be effective within industry parameters. It stresses quality aspects and it includes small tangible deliverables, together with the precise control of the project progress.

These agile software methodologies do not use strict phases but they include a series of recommendations which aim at easing up the development [1, 11]. In addition, they substitute the strict documentation for an intense level of communication among clients and developers. However, the lack of time from clients and the problems of communication and coordination noted in previous projects jeopardize these development approaches. Besides, they have been proven inappropriate for developments in which the team members work in an asynchronous and distributed way. The following section presents the SSP methodology, which has been specifically designed to support small-size software development projects in the above mentioned scenario.

4. The Simple Software Process

The Simple Software Process (SSP) proposed in this paper intends to be appropriate enough to support the development of small information systems, in immature scenarios. The first version of this process was defined in 1998 to support software development projects carried out by computer science undergraduate students at the Pontificia Universidad Católica de Chile.

The course where this experience took place was ICC2152 - Software Engineering Laboratory (10th term). In this course, students are grouped in teams and one role is assigned to each member. Responsibilities and rights of each role are specified in SSP. During 16 weeks the teams develop a real software application and interact with real clients and users. Over fifty small-size projects have been developed using SSP.

Since 2001, SSP has been also applied in the Universidad de Chile, in a course similar to the previously mentioned one. This work reports only the last twenty-two projects which have been carried out by undergraduate and graduate students from Universidad de Chile, in the course CC51A – Software Engineering (10th term), which keeps the same development scenario.

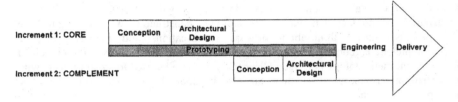

Fig. 1. Structure of SSP model

This development process involves two increments (Core and Complement) and each one is composed of four phases (Figure 1): *conception, architectural design, engineering* and *delivery*. The reason to propose two increments is because past experiences have shown that controlled two-steps approaches provide good results in short-time projects.

The first increment involves about 70% of user requirements and 100% of quality requirements. The second increment addresses the residual user requirements, which usually are not clear by the time the project starts. Thus, delays because unclear and changing requirements are reduced. The requirements of the second increment should be aligned with those defined in the first increment. Otherwise, a negotiation instance will be required.

Usually, the time spent in the development of the first and second increment is also around 70% and 30% respectively. The SSP approach involves a little work of integration, which has not relevant impact on the project schedule. In addition, the products to be integrated have been conceived and specified for fast integration. It allows developers to work asynchronously and in a distributed way avoiding delays caused by unclear requirements.

Furthermore, the prototyping during the development is a service that supports each phase in order to make it agile, improve the quality of the obtained products, and reduce the anxiety of clients. The next section describes the SSP phases and the dynamics of the development process. After it, section 4.2 presents a brief description of the roles involved in the development.

4.1. Phases of the model

In contrast to other development methodologies, the parallel work with low interactions among team members is fundamental in SSP. The restrictions on development time force team members to optimize the process, by maintaining low interaction among them, and working in an asynchronous/distributed way. In the following sub-section, the four phases of SSP are presented.

Conception. This stage has two goals: (1) to define the project viability, and —if it turns to be viable— (2) to specify the user requirements which will guide the development process. The project viability is identified through an effort estimation methodology called CWADEE (Chilean Web Application Development Effort Estimation) [14]. If the project turns viable, the collected information is used to design the elicitation process, which has two stages. The first stage is oriented to capturing the most important and stable user requirements. With this information, the developer may create prototypes that are used to verify, validate and redefine such requirements with the user-clients. The second stage is oriented to capture those requirements that are contradictory, conflictive or not clear enough. The prototype developed for the first stage is updated in order to support the prototype revisions with users and clients. Typically, these two stages are enough to identify the user requirements. Then, if needed, the development effort estimation could be adjusted. Finally, a User Requirement Document (URD) is created and validated through rapid prototypes. This document, like other ones proposed by SSP, is clearly specified and it is simple to write. Furthermore, during this phase, a set of test cases is built and documented in TCD.

Architectural Design. The inputs to this phase are the URD and the last prototype of the system. The phase main goal is to define the product structure in terms of subsystems, relationship among subsystems, information structure, system navigation and basic look-and-feel. It also specifies the operational environment of the system. This information is included in the Architectural Design Document (ADD) which is the result of this phase. During this stage programmers work in parallel with designers, by having these latter ones keep the coordination of activities and process control. Thus, when this phase ends, the obtained prototype is used to test the designed architecture with users and clients. Such prototype includes the look-and-feel, the navigation pattern and the raw functionality of the system.

Engineering. This phase uses the ADD to generate a detailed design that is implemented directly on the current prototype. The usability is the motivation for this phase, and the main goal is to get a product that is usable. During the development of the first increment, the programmers implement as much as possible in order to reduce the risks and to validate the usability of the Web application. During the second phase, the additional functionality is implemented, and both the complex functionality and the component integration are carried out. Eventually, some designers can participate in this phase as consultants in order to ensure the product usability. Upon finishing this phase, a usable product meeting the increment requirements should be obtained.

Delivery. The delivery phase is focused on installing the product in the user/client premises, to evaluate the acceptation level and to carry out minor adjustments if necessary. This phase is short and it is in charge of the programmers.

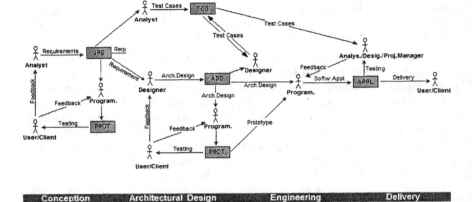

Fig. 2. Example of SSP dynamics

Figure 2 shows the dynamics of an SSP increment. The diagram shows three cycles in which it is possible to do testing and get feedback from the clients/users/team members. The first cycle is related to the conception phase, the next one is related to the architectural design phase and the last one is related to engineering. The process dynamics can be adjusted according to team member skills and roles that are present in the team work.

4.2. The roles

SSP demands for six roles to be assigned to group members: *project manager, analyst, designer, programmer, tester* and *user/client.* Although the user and client are not formally part of the work team, they play a key role during the development in order to help accomplishing the project scheduling. SSP formally proposes to include this role in the development process as a way to assure a quantum of user/client's time. Experiences using SPP indicates that it is a key factor to consider in order to have normal project execution. The formal participation of users/clients allows them to be conscious of their responsibilities. Moreover, the rest of team members are conscious of the user/client's role and the formal interactions required with these new members of the team. Provided that roles and interactions among the participants are well specified, a common understanding is created and maintained during the execution of the project. It increases the project visibility for all people involved in the development.

A team member could play a maximum of two roles during the project in order to avoid bottlenecks. However, just some roles combinations are recommended. For example, it is not recommended that a person may have the roles of programmer and tester, because testers have to review the programmers' work. Next, a brief description of the roles considered in SSP is presented.

Analyst. The analysts are responsible for the conception phase. They have to (1) establish if the project is viable or not, and (2) specify the user requirements in the URD (User Requirements Document). This document is a simplified version of the ESA Software Engineering Standard proposal [5]. The analyst-programmer or analyst-tester role combinations have shown to be appropriate if a person has to play more than one role.

Designer. The designers are in charge of the architectural design phase, which produces the ADD (Architectural Design Document). It includes the architectural design of the software application and operational environment. Moreover, it includes the design of the application look-and-feel and navigation. Designers also collaborate with the programmer during the engineering phase by testing and improving the product usability. Besides, they can adjust or add test cases to TCD (Test Cases Document). A person whose main role is designer can also play a programmer or tester role.

Programmer. The programmers are in charge of the engineering phase. They are responsible for the development of fast prototypes to be shown and the final product. Usually, they participate during the architectural design phase in order to assure that designs may be quickly implemented. A person whose main role is programmer can also play an analyst or designer role.

Tester. The tester is usually a distributed role, which is played by several members along the development process. For example, analysts can play a tester role when the conception phase has concluded. This role is responsible for specifying the test cases and for checking whether the products adhere to the specifications. Typically, the tester generates the TCD and reports the testing processes. The process presented in Figure 2 shows roles that can also act as tester during each phase of an increment.

Project Manager. The project manager plans, coordinates and controls the activities of the team members. The manager can also act as tester during part of the process and he/she typically acts as a communication interface with the client/user.

User/Client. The users and clients are in charge of (1) providing information and requirements of system to be developed, and (2) providing feedback to developers about the interim products that are delivered during the process. The software developers have internal check points with the users and clients every week in order to diagnose the project advance. Such meetings are formally scheduled and they take 10-20 minutes. Attendance to these meeting is part of the duties of users and clients.

Experiments performed in two Chilean universities are presented below. The experimentation scenario is similar to the one characterized in section 2.The obtained results are not conclusive enough; however they show the web development process in immature scenarios can be controlled in order to be predictable.

5. Experimental Results

Various versions of SSP have been used in more than 50 projects since 1998. This paper reports only the 22 last projects which show the results of the SSP current version. This software process has been used to support software development in software engineering courses taught at two major Chilean universities: Pontificia Universidad Católica de Chile and Universidad de Chile.

Typically, these courses are taken by advanced undergraduate and graduate students of computer science. As previously mentioned, students are grouped in teams of 4-6 people. Each team member had to play at least a role, by considering that all SSP roles must be covered. Then, a real project is assigned to each team. The projects involved participation of real clients and users. Although the scope and main requirements of the projects were previously agreed between instructors and clients, the team members had to negotiate the projects scope with their clients in order to make effective the developers estimations. Each team had 16 weeks to develop and deliver the final product.

At start time, the work teams had to define SSP adaptation to conduct the development process. The communication/coordination infrastructure supporting the team members included email, telephone, a CVS (Concurrent Versions System) and a document describing the roles and the interaction protocol. Students were free to use these or other coordination tools.

Instructors defined three main check points for each project execution: upon finishing the conception phase during first increment, upon ending the conception phase during the second increment, and upon completing the engineering phase during both increments (core and complement). In order to diagnose the projects advance, a formal technical review was conducted during each check point. The reviews took 60-90 minutes by project. These instances were used to get part of the results reported in table 1.

Results shown in Table 1 correspond to those obtained in software projects developed from first term 2003 to second term 2005. In order to present the results the projects were classified by the instructors according to size and complexity, based on the amount and complexity of user requirements. The following project categories were identified: Very Small size - Medium complexity (VSM), Very Small size – Complex (VSC), Small Size – Low complexity (SSL), Small Size – Medium complexity (SSM). For each project category, it is presented:

  a) the number of initiated projects,

  b) the number of projects under production -successfully finished- ,

  c) the number of members per work team,

  d) the average and standard deviation of the spent man-hours,

  e) the average and standard deviation of clients'/users' assessments about the obtained product,

  f) the average and standard deviation of team members' assessments about SSP as support for the development process,

g) the average and standard deviation of the experts' assessments about the quality of the final product,

h) the average and standard deviation of the team members' assessments about visibility of the project provided by SSP, and

i) the average and standard deviation of the clients/users' assessments about visibility of the project during the development process.

The two first assessments (items e and f) were carried out by using questionnaires designed with the method proposed by Zapata et al. [22], and the third assessments (item g) was done using an extension of the 8-issues questionnaire proposed by Nielsen [13]. The values range between 1 and 10, the higher the better.

Results show the SSP is predictable in terms of time, because most projects were completed and put into production. The man-hour values are stable enough according to project types as to support realistic estimations, regardless of the team work. The clients' and experts' assessments indicate that good quality products can be obtained. The work teams' opinions show a high level of satisfaction when using SSP to guide the development process. The same occurs with the project visibility as seen by clients/users and team members. The low clients/users commitment was the common factor in those projects that were not put into production.

Table 1. Experimental results

Item	Category/Issues	VSM	VSC	SSL	SSM
A	Number of Projects	4	6	7	5
B	Number of Completed Projects	3	5	7	4
C	People by Work Team	4	5 – 6	4 - 5	5 – 6
D	Man Hours / Standard Deviation	248 / 35	367 / 71	285 / 32	389 / 68
E	Clients-Users Assessment / Std. Deviation	8.5 / 0.7	8.2 / 0.9	8.9 / 0.8	8.7 /1.2
F	Work Team Assessment / Std. Deviation	8.5 / 0.5	9.1 / 0.7	9.1 / 0.6	9.4 / 0.5
G	Expert Assessment / Std. Deviation	8.0 / 0.7	8.3 / 0.5	7.9 / 0.3	8.2 / 0.4
H	Team Members Visibility / Std. Deviation	8.7 / 0.4	8.5 / 0.5	9.2 / 0.4	9.1 / 0.6
I	Clients-Users Visibility / Std. Deviation	9.1 / 0.3	8.0 / 0.4	9.3 / 0.5	9.2 / 0.3

On the other hand, SSP has been applied to three projects out of the university scenario, in a small software company. They were two SSL and one SSM project. The obtained results reported by the project manager were similar to those shown on Table 1.

The main strengths of SSP are their simplicity and clarity about roles to play (including the client/user), tasks to be done and interactions between activities. These interactions, allows team members to work in an asynchronous and distributed way.

Observing the results we can say that SSP provides a good visibility of the project for both developers and users/clients and produces predictable results. These features make SSP appropriate to support developments of small-size software projects in immature scenarios.

6. Conclusions and Future Work

Usually, small-size software projects carried out in immature development scenarios cannot guarantee either the development time and cost or the quality of the final product. The limitations that well-known heavyweight and lightweight software methodologies have to guide developments in such a scenario were presented in section 3.

In order to deal with this problem, authors have studied several software projects in Chile to identify key issues that are the source for most problems. The results showed a poor understanding or consideration of key issues such as: rights and duties of team members' roles, development context, process activities, coordination protocols, users/clients participation and project visibility. SSP has taken these issues into account. It evolutions has been guided by the lessons learned with each project. The results obtained of its application in 22 projects are encouraging. SSP seems to be a viable alternative to guide small-size software development in immature scenarios.

This proposal is based on the cases we had at hand. We do not know yet its extensibility to other cultural settings. This will be the subject of a forthcoming paper. However, it is possible to hypothesize its applicability to similar cultural and economical environments such as other Latin-American countries.

In the short term, we will continue testing SSP in the reported scenario, and we will start testing such a methodology within software companies. In the long term, we plan to use SSP in several software developments settings in order to identify its limitations.

Acknowledgements

This work has been partially supported by grants N° 1030959 and 1040952 from Fondecyt (Chile).

References

[1] K. Beck. Extreme Programming Explained. Addison-Wesley, 2000.
[2] B. Bohem. A Spiral Model for Software Development and Enhancement. IEEE Computer, Vol. 21, No. 5, 61-72. 1988.
[3] A. Cockburn. Agile Software Development. Adisson-Wesley, 2002.
[4] O. DeTroyer and K. Leune. WSDM: a User Centered Design Method for Web Sites. Proc. of the Int. 7th World-Wide Web Conference, Brisbane, Australia. 1998.

[5] European Space Agency. ESA Software Engineering Standards. PSS-05-0 Issue 2. ESA Board for Software Standardization and Control (BSSC). February, 1991.

[6]   M.   Fowler.   The   New   Methodology.   April   2003. http://www.martinfowler.com/articles/newMethodology.html.

[7] M. Gaedke, D. Schempf and H. Gellersen. WCML: An Enabling Technology for the Reuse in Object-Oriented Web Engineering. Proc. of 8th Int. World Wide Web Conference (WWW8). Toronto, Ontario, Canada. 1999.

[8] M. Gaedke and G. Graef. Development and Evolution of Web-Applications using the WebComposition Process Model. Proc. of Int. Workshop on Web Engineering at the WWW9, Amsterdam, The Netherlands, May 2000.

[9] F. Guerrero. Success Factors for Adopting and International Process Standard in a Chilean Software Organization: An Experimental Study. Master Thesis. DCC. Universidad Catolica de Chile. Santiago, Chile. May, 2003.

[10] IDC Chile. The Chilean Software Industry. A Study for Japan External Trade Organization (in Spanish). International Data Corporation Chile (IDC Chile). 2003.

[11] R. Jeffries, A. Anderson, and C. Hendrickson. Extreme Programming Installed. Addison-Wesley, 2001.

[12] P. Kruchten. The Rational Unified Process- An Introduction. Third Edition. Addison-Wesley. 2004.

[13] J. Nielsen. Usability Engineering. Academic Press, London, 1993.

[14] S. Ochoa, M.C. Bastarrica. CWADEE: A Chilean Web Application Development Effort Estimation Process. In Proceedings of LA-Web 2003 Conference. IEEE Press. Santiago, Chile. 10-12 November, 2003.

[15] S. Palmer and M. Felsing. A Practical Guide to Feature-Driven Development. Prentice Hall, 2002.

[16] R. Pressman. Software Engineering: A Practitioner's Approach. 5th Edition, McGraw Hill. 2000.

[17] E. Sacre. A Methodology To Develop Web Applications in Small and Medium Size Enterprises (in Spanish). Master Thesis. Computer Science Department, University of Chile. June, 2003.

[18] D. Schwabe, G. Rossi, S, Barbosa. Systematic Hypermedia Design with OOHDM. Proceedings of the International Conference on Hypertext' 96. Washington, USA. 1996.

[19] K. Schwaber. The Scrum Development Process. Proceedings of OOPSLA '95, Workshop on Business Object Design and Implementation, Austin, Texas, USA. ACM Press. October 1995.

[20] D. Schwabe, G. Rossi, S, Barbosa. An Object Oriented Approach to Web-Based Applications Design. In: TAPOS – Theory And Practice of Object Systems, 207-225. 1998.

[21] W. Stein. A Web Software Process for Small or Medium-Sized Projects Focused on the Chilean Scenario. Engineering Thesis (In Spanish). Computer Science Department, Universidad de Chile, April 2003.

[22] S. Zapata, M. Lund. Proposal to Measure Software Customers Satisfaction. Proceedings of 1st Argentine Symposium on Software Engineering (ASSE' 2000), Tandil, Argentina. pp.185-197. September 4-9. 2000.

A Method for Collaborative Requirements Elicitation and Decision-Supported Requirements Analysis

Michael Geisser and Tobias Hildenbrand

University of Mannheim, Schloss, 68131 Mannheim, Germany,
{geisser, hildenbrand}@uni-mannheim.de,
WWW home page: http://wifo1.bwl.uni-mannheim.de/team.html

Abstract. As software systems become more and more complex with a multitude of stakeholders involved in development activities, novel ways of conducting the process of requirements elicitation and analysis are to be found. Therefore, this paper introduces a method for collaborative requirements elicitation and decision-supported requirements analysis. Accompanying this method, appropriate tools and techniques, both existing and custom-made, are referred to. The method is designed for a geographically distributed collaborative environment in order to support software manufacturers as well as IT departments which develop software solutions for multiple users or even consortiums of customers.

1 Introduction

Since the '60s, numerous methods for a more systematic approach to software development have been devised as part of the newly created software engineering (SE) discipline. SE in general aims at consistently producing high-quality software within predictable budget restrictions and project schedules. However, even today surveys show that the majority of all software projects significantly run out of schedule and budget. This and further problems in software projects are mostly caused by a lack of understanding of the customers' needs at the beginning of the project as well as by unsystematic approaches to early development activities [14, 24, 25]. The discipline of requirements engineering (RE) focuses on these early stages of software development projects.

Introducing a more systematic method for RE constitutes a fundamental prerequisite for realizing the goals of SE. This task is even more complicated when

Please use the following format when citing this chapter:

Geisser, M., Hildenbrand, T., 2006, in IFIP International Federation for Information Processing, Volume 219, Advanced Software Engineering: Expanding the Frontiers of Software Technology, eds. Ochoa, S., Roman, G.-C., (Boston: Springer), pp. 108–122.

considering consortiums of multiple customers: This implies the involvement of numerous stakeholders from different organizations. In this particular scenario, it is of high importance to systematically guide the stakeholders with their respective opinions through the RE process in order to reach a consensus which the consequent stages of SE can build upon.

In an aim to support software manufacturers in addressing these complications, this paper provides a theoretically sound method accompanied by appropriate tools for collaborative requirements elicitation including decision support for requirements analysis. The CoREA method (Collaborative Requirements Elicitation and Analysis) aims at enabling software companies to systematically elicit requirements in a distributed environment and provides profound and objective decision support for analyzing and selecting relevant requirements.

After having already outlined the paper's underlying problem statement and objective, an overview and critical evaluation of related RE approaches and methods will be given as theoretical framework. Section 3 contains a description of the method consisting of two major parts: (a) eliciting a complete set of requirements with regards to a distributed collaborative scenario and (b) analyzing those requirements in order to find a reasonable and objective choice for implementation. Supportive tools for each step of the method will also be presented. The concluding section summarizes the results of our research, including a demarcation to previous work, and provides an outlook on future research questions.

2   Related Work

As already indicated, most problems in software development stem from a poor initial understanding of the customers' needs. RE deals with this difficulty and tries to systematically create a better understanding in the early stages of a SE project. The most common definition of the RE process is that of Ian Sommerville: "The requirements for a system are the descriptions of the services provided by the system and its operational constraints. [...] The process of finding out, analysing, documenting and checking these services and constraints is called requirements engineering" [23]. This process is subdivided into four phases, namely feasibility study, requirements elicitation and analysis, requirements specification, and requirements validation. Parallel and subsequent to these phases, requirements management covers all activities concerning the management of emerging changes to requirements during the whole software development process [23].

2.1   Collaborative Requirements Engineering

As Cook und Churcher observed, „Software Engineering is inherently a team-based activity" [6], and thus, SE, and RE in particular, are not feasible without a certain degree of collaboration, in most cases. Moreover, involving all relevant stakeholders early on in the process is particularly crucial for successful software projects [2]. Among all RE phases, requirements elicitation and analysis is an especially collaborative stage: first, stakeholders from both the software company and the customer need to be identified, and second, requirements from all these stakeholders have to be gathered collaboratively. In particular, requirements analysis takes place among stakeholders from the ordering party supported by the software vendor. Requirements specification is carried out collaboratively as well: the pivotal activity (modeling), can only be successful after continuous consultation with the customers' stakeholders. Many computer scientists advocate an even deeper involvement of all stakeholders within the requirements specification phase by means of collaborative methods [1, 9]. The remaining phases of RE are by far less collaborative than the two previously mentioned. In the following, existing approaches to collaborative requirements elicitation and analysis will be the center of attention.

2.2   Collaborative Requirements Elicitation and Analysis

Considering scientific approaches for collaborative requirements elicitation and analysis, there is only one established research endeavor, namely the WinWin approach. Originating from Boehm's Theory W [5], WinWin has evolved over four iterations from an extended spiral model of software development [4] to the latest version, called EasyWinWin (EWW) [10]. This approach propagates a change from traditional, contract-oriented mechanisms to collaborative practices based on trustful relationships among stakeholders. EWW does not aim at rigid agreements and detailed requirements specifications. It rather tries to provide the stakeholders involved with a shared vision and common beliefs in order to be able to react to both unforeseen problems and opportunities in an adaptive and quick manner [3]. The establishment of trust among all team members is an integral constituent of the EWW method. Additionally, this approach leads to more realistic expectations among stakeholders, since they exchange and scrutinize their respective beliefs by means of intensive discourse. Moreover, EWW is able to reveal tacit knowledge as well as conflicts and inconsistencies in very early stages of the requirements elicitation and analysis phase [12]. Other advantageous features of this method include its detailed process description, which provides certainty and guidance for participating stakeholders, as well as its supportive groupware tools. Thus, EWW combines the WinWin spiral model of SE with collaborative knowledge techniques and automation of a custom-built group support system [5].

The relatively high complexity constitutes the major downside of this approach since the process is not very intuitional and necessitates training for both moderators and participants. Moreover, the process is not tailored to a distributed environment as physical discussions are a fundamental element of the method. The relatively high subjectivity of requirements selection accounts for another disadvantage. Although EWW tries to guarantee a certain degree of objectiveness by means of a prioritization mechanism, the absolute character of this mechanism is inferior to comparative ones [15]. Another drawback is the "ease of realization" criterion for assessing requirements. Since this criterion incorporates numerous factors it is arguable whether all stakeholders are capable of rating this property on an absolute scale. The directive not to vote unless stakeholders feel able to assess this criterion is also problematic, since the participants' subjective appraisement may differ significantly from their actual abilities. Table 1 provides an overview of EWW's advantages and disadvantages in context of our initial problem statement.

Table 1. Evaluation of the EasyWinWin method

Advantages	Disadvantages
+ Flexibility	- Not very intuitional
+ Establishment of trust	- Not suitable for distributed development
+ Realistic expectations	- Relatively high subjectivity
+ Revelation of tacit knowledge	
+ Early detection of conflicts	
+ Detailed process description	
+ Tool support (groupware)	

2.3   Distributed Requirements Elicitation and Analysis

The gradual globalization of economies makes highly distributed software development techniques indispensable. The driving force and rationale behind this development is the opportunity to share resources and to use wage differentials on a global scale. Against this background, not only the distributed SE process as a whole has been subject to researchers' investigations [1] but also distributed RE, and particularly requirements elicitation, has been studied empirically [7, 8, 13]. However, these studies unanimously deal with distributed elicitation activities using traditional techniques and methods not necessarily suitable for distributed environments. Furthermore, many asynchronous techniques (e.g. shared glossaries and discussion forums) are not explicitly taken into consideration. However, all studies deem distributed requirements elicitation possible and even favorable compared to collocated approaches. In order to realize this potential advantage, methodical principles need to be taken into consideration and requirements for tool support have to be granted. E.g. initial face-to-face meetings are considered essential in order to establish trustful relationships among the persons involved [8]. Important requirements for collaborative tools include support for both synchronous and asynchronous collaboration capabilities [13].

With regards to EWW's original groupware, geographically distributed stakeholders were only integrated in a rudimental way. Therefore, a web-based tool for distributed requirements elicitation supporting the EWW approach was developed: ARENA [11]. However, this tool does not complement the existing groupware tools but replaces them. Therefore, in order to conduct collaborative, distributed requirements elicitation and analysis, the whole process has to be run within the boundaries of the ARENA tool. This, in turn, is very problematic, since ARENA solely supports web-based asynchronous collaboration. Thus, it is impossible to arrange synchronous meetings which play a pivotal role within the original method. Besides ARENA, two other applications supporting EWW were developed especially for mobile devices. Thus, it is possible not only to conduct requirements elicitation in a geographically distributed setting but also without any tie to fixed desktop workplaces. These mobile tools are especially useful in scenarios where collocated workshops are held in combination with interviewing geographically distributed stakeholders [22].

Open source software development (OSSD) constitutes another source of insight into techniques for distributed requirements elicitation and analysis. In OSSD, the overall development process is primarily distributed. Therefore, further findings for the course of this paper can be derived – especially when considering the major downsides of EWW, namely being non-intuitional and not suitable for distributed environments. However, major differences between commercial software projects and OSSD can be found, in particular when comparing requirements processes. Unlike commercial developers, open source developers are mostly among the future users of the software product [17]. Empirical studies reveal that requirements processes in OSSD projects run much more implicitly and informally than in any other kind of development project – sometimes even omitting some of the generally accepted RE activities [17, 21]. In particular, requirements elicitation and analysis is carried out much more informally than in traditional RE, as requirements are elicited, elaborated, and discussed in forums and via mailing lists. Especially in case of distributed environments, forums represent an efficient way of asynchronously eliciting requirements even in commercial settings – particularly in terms of resource consumption. However, these forums should be structured and supervised by a moderator, in order to coach those stakeholders not so familiar with the medium and to run the process as systematically as possible.

2.4   Quantitative Approaches to Requirements Engineering

The RE process has to consider various requests from diverse stakeholders, each having a different view on the system to be built and thus having varying priorities. Furthermore, most stakeholders are unaware of the implementation costs of the respective requirements. Due to budget restrictions, it is generally impossible to incorporate all the stakeholders' requirements in the final software product. Therefore, a reasonable selection has to be conducted in order to maximize customer value [19]. In the literature, two major methods supporting quantitative RE can be found: the Cost-Value Approach [15], and Quantitative WinWin [18, 19]. Both methods base upon the Analytic Hierarchy Process (AHP) [20], a supportive method for complex team decision processes which has proved to be superior to other requirements prioritization algorithms in RE [16].

The **Cost-Value Approach** (CVA) features intuitional and easy handling. In addition, this method leads to better results than absolute ones due to its solid mathematical foundation. The AHP's pairwise comparisons have a detrimental effect, since the method's complexity rises exponentially compared to the number of requirements. Neither are possible interdependencies between requirements considered [15]. Thus, e.g. a requirement with a very low value-cost ratio might be indispensable for implementing another requirement with a very high value-cost ratio. The CVA would advise to omit this indispensable requirement, even though the global maximum of customer value could thus never be attained.

Quantitative WinWin (QWW), on the other hand, considerably reduces the number of comparisons by using the AHP hierarchically [18]. However, the effect of the AHP's pairwise comparisons still has a negative impact on the process, since several iterations are extremely demanding in terms of the stakeholders' cooperation and willingness to participate. Therefore, QWW is still more complex than the CVA. It also features a solid mathematical foundation and thus overcomes the limitations of a subjective requirements selection. The stakeholders' cooperation is even more mission-critical when evaluating the relative importance of requirements as proposed in the extended version of this approach [19]. Nevertheless, the method's original assumption that the relative importance values of requirements are given has to be considered quite unrealistic. Moreover, when estimating costs (as well as duration and quality in the extended version) using the proposed simulation system represents more of a risk than an improvement, since the expected quality of results from this estimation is at least arguable [19]. Furthermore, neither consistency checks of the stakeholders' AHP comparisons nor interdependent requirements are taken into consideration. These interdependencies are particularly crucial, since it can be assumed that both value and complexity of respective requirements will not stay constant but will rise with a growing number of implemented features [19]. Finally, the method's name is somehow misleading, because it has nothing in common with the original WinWin approach but the iterative nature of the process. Table 2 outlines the results of the quantitative methods' evaluation.

Table 2. Comparison of Cost-Value Approach and Quantitative WinWin

Method	Advantages	Disadvantages
Cost-Value Approach	+ Mathematical foundation + Cost-value consideration + Consistency check + Intuitional handling	- No consideration of interdependencies among requirements - Complexity
Quantitative WinWin	+ Mathematical foundation + Cost-value consideration + Hierarchical AHP	- No consideration of interdependencies among requirements - High complexity - No consistency check - Cost estimate problematic - Close cooperation among stakeholders needed

3 Introducing the CoREA method

Based on the analysis and evaluation of existing approaches, we now introduce the CoREA method for collaborative RE. CoREA covers collaborative requirements elicitation in a distributed environment as well as quantitative decision support for distributed requirements prioritization and selection. The CoREA method consists of two distinct phases: Phase I is predominantly concerned with the iterative and collaborative elicitation of requirements from different stakeholders, while explicitly taking into account geographically distributed work. Subsequently, in phase II, costs and values of the respective requirements are analyzed in order to support the selection process with regards to the ensuing design and implementation phases.

3.1   Collaborative Requirements Elicitation

In phase I of the CoREA method, requirements are elicited both collaboratively and iteratively. The method builds upon EWW but uses techniques from OSSD in order to achieve both a more intuitional procedure and consistent support for distributed collaboration. The objective of this first phase is to capture the requirements as completely as possible. Hence, a vague vision conceptualizing the customers' needs serves as starting input. Moreover, an initial list of relevant stakeholders must be available. The set of relevant stakeholders as well as the central vision evolves over time, as several iterations of the process will be traversed. The respective process steps for CoREA's collaborative requirements elicitation phase will be described in detail in the following sections.

Step 1:   Initial Meeting

Within the scope of the initial meeting the vision statement along with a first list of stakeholders is handed over to the software company. This meeting enables the establishment of interpersonal relationships among the stakeholders who are supposed to collaborate predominantly asynchronously and geographically distributed within the following steps.

Step 2:   Brainstorming

Asynchronous brainstorming aims at generating first ideas about the software to be developed in the project. Web-based forums are utilized to enable geographically distributed collaboration among stakeholders. Thus, they are able to generate new ideas as well as complement and comment existing entries. Whereas criticism during brainstorming sessions is often interdicted, CoREA prescribes this explicitly in order to reject unrealistic requirements as soon as possible in the RE process. This second step is supposed to be supported intensely by a moderator from the software manufacturer who supervises and adjusts the detail level of discussion, if necessary. Furthermore, the moderator ensures the correct and consistent usage of technical terms, e.g. by systematically asking questions. In addition, he fosters active participation of all stakeholders by purposefully addressing people.

Step 3:   Revise Vision and Identify Categories

After having completed the brainstorming step, the vision document has to be revised by the moderator and a further SE expert from the software company. Their task is to incorporate the ideas previously generated in step 2. In addition, categories for upcoming requirements need to be identified from the given sets of ideas in order to guarantee a structured procedure in the subsequent steps. At the same time, a SE expert tries to identify and reject unrealistic proposals and thus ensures the system's realizability and technical feasibility. Moreover, the expert detects technical terms, which have to be defined in a common glossary.

Step 4:   Prioritize Categories & Discussion

The prioritization of requirement categories and subsequent discussion occurs within the scope of a virtual meeting. Alongside the moderator who guides all participants through the process and all stakeholders provided by the customer, the SE expert from step 3 also has to participate in this meeting. In order to realize such a virtual meeting, multimedia-based groupware is necessary. In particular, audio and video conferencing as well as anonymous polling features are vital for conducting this step. At first, the proposals rejected in step 3 will be paid attention to and the SE expert has to justify their exclusion. Afterwards, the stakeholders have to conduct an anonymous prioritization of requirement categories. In doing so, each category's importance has to be assessed from the customers' organizations' points of view on a scale ranging from 0 (not important at all) up to 3 (extremely important). A more detailed graduation of the scale would not be appropriate at this point, since the stakeholders' perceptions are still relatively imprecise and significant differences in categorization are yet to be detected. In case of substantial differences in the stakeholders' assessments of particular categories the meaning and the relevance of this category have to be discussed intensely. This discussion aims at reaching a consensus among all stakeholders involved. After the discussion, the moderator presents the revised vision and incorporates further changes if necessary. The list of technical terms identified for the glossary will also be shown and, if required, complemented by further terms. This step concludes by deciding whether new stakeholders have to be involved for the ongoing course of the elicitation process and which of the current stakeholders are dispensable for the time being.

Step 5: Create or Revise Glossary

The creation of the glossary containing technical terms identified in the previous steps is supposed to be conducted asynchronously and geographically distributed. For this purpose, a web-based technology, e.g. a Wiki system or comparable groupware systems allowing collaborative, asynchronous document editing over the Internet, can be utilized.

Step 6: Submit and Comment Requirements

Again, a structured web-enabled discussion forum is utilized in order to be able to both submit new and comment on existing requirements asynchronously and from different geographic locations. In this forum, the moderator creates different areas for the respective requirement categories as well as one additional area for requirements that could not have been categorized so far. As in step 2, the moderator tries to resolve ambiguities by asking questions, requests more precise explanations and fosters active participation by all stakeholders.

Step 7: Consolidate and Categorize Requirements

In this step, the requirements submitted and annotated via the discussion forum have to be consolidated by the moderator and the SE expert from the software manufacturer. Thereby, all findings from the respective discussion threads have to be merged. After that, these consolidated requirements are allocated either to existing categories or newly created ones. While allocating requirements the SE expert pays attention to the fact that interdependent requirements are not classified in different categories. He also tries to identify and eliminate proposals for unrealistic requirements. In addition he compiles technical terms to be specified in the glossary. If necessary, the vision might be revised and adapted as well.

Step 8: Prioritize Categories and Requirements & Discussion

In order to collaborate effectively in terms of costs and time consumption as well as to establish trust and interpersonal relationships among stakeholders, organizing alternating physical and virtual meetings is a promising approach. Thus, in case step 8 has to be traversed several times and the most recent meeting was a virtual one, the following iteration demands for a physical meeting. This step is conducted analogously to step 4. However, besides prioritizing and discussing categories, requirements themselves are also to be dealt with at this point. In case the glossary has to be revised or new stakeholders have been identified, another iteration starting with step 5 has to be traversed. Otherwise, all participants check the categories in terms of completeness. If there are uncompleted categories, another partial iteration traversing steps 5 to 8 is required. If no further iterations are required, the phase I of CoREA is considered completed. Figure 1 depicts a spiral model of the requirements elicitation process in order to visualize the method's iterative character and contextualize the respective steps.

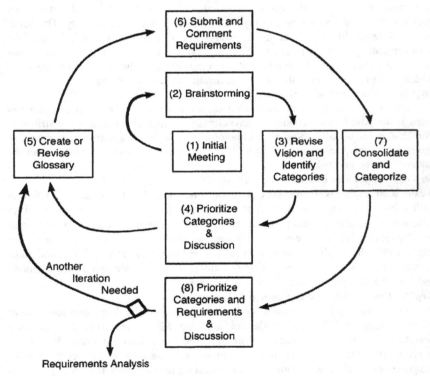

Fig. 1. CoREA Spiral Model of Collaborative Requirements Elicitation

3.2   Decision-Supported Requirements Analysis

Within the second phase of the CoREA method, requirements are selected for actual implementation based upon a quantitative analysis of costs and customer value. The starting point of this process is a list of requirements, as it was gathered and consolidated during the requirements elicitation phase. From an economic point of view, implementing only those requirements providing satisfactory value as compared to their costs is considered reasonable. Monetary budget restrictions can also necessitate a more deliberate selection of requirements. Thereby, this selection is conducted according to the value-cost ratio: the requirements with the highest ratios will be implemented.

Step 1:   Form Requirements Sets

Since requirements always bear interdependencies among each other, they cannot be compared in a way that neglects these interdependencies. If one or more categories (cp. section 3.1) contain interdependent requirements, so-called requirements sets have to be formed. Figure 2 shows a graphical representation of interdependent requirements and requirements sets. In this example, requirement A2 is a prerequisite for A3. The latter, together with A0, is in turn a precondition for A4 and A5. Taken together the directed graph forms a self-contained requirements set. A1 does not depend on any other requirements and thus forms a set of its own. Requirements set 3 consists of two interdependent requirements B1 and B2 and the implementation of the former is a prerequisite for the latter.

Step 2:   Estimate Costs and Values

As soon as the requirements sets have been formed within the different categories, costs and values for requirements and requirements sets have to be estimated. While the software company's SE expert is exclusively responsible for realistic cost estimations, estimating the requirements' value is up to the stakeholders provided by the customers. Costs are estimated on the one hand on a quantity basis (e.g. by man-days) and on the other hand on a value basis (e.g. daily rate per employee). Customer value is determined by means of the AHP (see section 2.4).

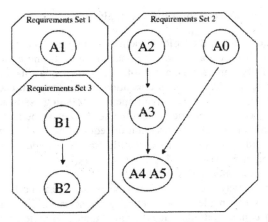

Fig. 2. Graphical Representation of Interdependencies

Step 3: Graphical Representation of Results
Results from step 2 are represented graphically with regards to interdependent requirements by depicting all possible combinations originating from root requirements in the directed graphs with their respective aggregated cost and value estimates. Figure 3 takes on the example given in step 1 (see Figure 2) displaying possible combinations of requirements. The diagram displays the different combinations and their respective cost-value characteristics. In order to support cost and value estimation especially for the CoREA method, a prototypical web application has been implemented. This prototype enables geographically distributed stakeholders to be securely guided through the estimation process. It implements the AHP algorithm and is able to visualize the results in the form of a cost-value diagram as shown in Figure 3 (see appendix).

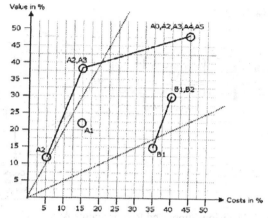

Fig. 3. CoREA Cost-Value Diagram

Step 4: Decide Upon Selection

Finally, a physical meeting of all stakeholders is conducted. The moderator presents the cost-value diagram with all possible requirements combinations and their cost and value estimations resulting from step 3. Based on this objectified foundation, it has to be decided which requirements will be implemented immediately, totally discarded, or preserved for upcoming releases. In order to provide additional decision support, the diagram contains two straight lines: requirements with at least two times more relative value than relative cost should be implemented in any case, whereas those with twice the relative costs should not be considered for implementation. These equations have been empirically tested and proven themselves suitable to distinguish preferable requirements with high value-cost ratios from those with a low ratio [15]. Finally, Figure 4 gives a visual overview of CoREA's requirements analysis phase. In combination with Figure 1 this depicts the overall CoREA method.

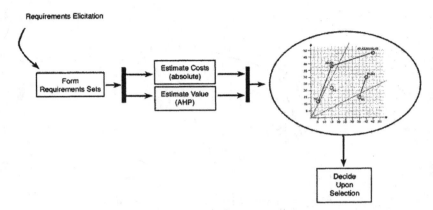

Fig. 4. Decision-Supported Requirements Analysis in CoREA

4   Conclusion

Based upon a critical evaluation of existing approaches, this paper introduces a novel, decision-supported method for collaborative requirements elicitation and analysis suitable for a distributed environment. This method consists of two subsequent phases. While requirements are elicited iteratively and as completely as possible in the first phase of the CoREA method, phase II provides methodic guidance for selecting those requirements that will actually be implemented. CoREA thus enables software manufacturers to systematically elicit the requirements collaboratively with customers in a distributed environment. This effect is achieved by transferring the established WinWin approach into a geographically distributed environment. Moreover, CoREA improves WinWin in terms of intuitional handling and objective requirements selection procedures. By enhancing WinWin's core properties, our method builds upon the vast theoretical and empirical knowledge gathered in the field of collaborative requirements elicitation. We are able to eliminate WinWin's well-known weaknesses through additional insights in the fields of distributed software development and quantitative methods for requirements evaluation. Besides enhancing EWW, CoREA for the first time takes interdependencies into account by introducing requirements sets as units of evaluation. This method and the tool prototype have been developed in close cooperation with the IT departments of two large German financial institutions.

To be able to gain additional empirical evidence, the method will be applied within several case studies. Since CoREA was developed within the scope of a larger research consortium, access to practical settings is ensured. Based on the practical experience from upcoming case studies, both tool support and the method itself will be improved and adapted.

Alongside prototypical evaluation, it is useful to complement CoREA through broadening the theoretical foundations. Even though it is deemed hard to design domain-specific methods for RE, it has yet to be analyzed, whether domain-specific process instances can be generated by means of ontologies and other semantic technologies. Moreover, requirements analysis and selection can be extended by time-related aspects as the current estimation of the requirements' costs and value might be complemented by taking development time into consideration. This in turn, is useful for process planning and control. Furthermore, the method's integrability with product line concepts in SE and traceability capabilities have to be analyzed in order to facilitate proactive reuse of requirements. Considering component-based software development methodologies, techniques for matching standard sets of requirements with standard infrastructure and business components are an open field of research as well.

In order to develop an integrated methodology for collaborative RE, future work also has to deal with adapting requirements specification and validation processes for distributed environments. Thus, the full potential of distribution, specialization and collaborative work can be exploited in the early stages of SE. Such an integrated methodology allows a better focus on the very early stages of SE. Hence, it provides a sound basis for inter-organizational division of labor, and faster realization of new software solutions. In doing so, higher quality is eventually achieved through the integration of multiple stakeholders with diverse competencies. In addition, an improved RE process leads to less consequential defects in later phases which become more expensive the later they emerge. The issues discussed in this paper do not only apply for RE but for the whole SE process and software lifecycle respectively. Enabling and improving distributed work, whether organizationally or geographically distributed, will play an important role in the course of the global industrialization process within the software sector. Therefore, considering the entire SE process, integrated methodic and technological support for collaborative software development projects are becoming more and more important in the future.

5   Appendix: Tool Prototype

In order to support cost and value estimation for requirements evaluation an internet-based prototype has been developed. This prototype is called IBERE (Internet-Based Empirical Requirements Evaluation) and guides distributed participants securely through the requirements estimation procedure. IBERE is also able to visualize the results of the requirements evaluation process in the form of a cost-value diagram by utilizing the AHP algorithm for calculating the utility value for each requirement. Thus, this prototype supports steps 2 and 3 of CoREA's decision-supported requirements analysis (cp. section 3.2). The screenshot in Figure 5 depicts pairwise comparisons of requirements within one set as part of the AHP procedure.

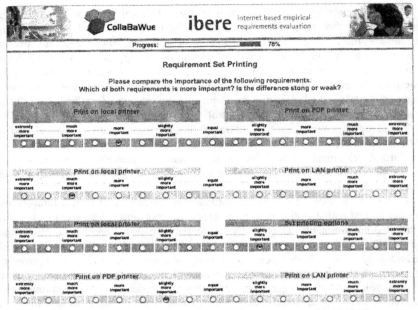

Fig. 5. Pairwise Comparison of Requirements with IBERE

Figure 6 depicts the graphical representation of the AHP's results (cp. step 3 in section 3.2). In this example, requirements 1.1, 1.3 and 2.1 should be implemented due to their high value-cost ratios, as indicated by their positions above the upper straight line. In contrast, the requirements 1.4 and 2.3 should not be taken into consideration for the final software product because of their unfavorable value-cost ratios. The consideration of requirements interdependencies (cp. Figures 2 and 3) in IBERE is currently under development and therefore cannot be shown in this screenshot.

Defining Security Requirements Through Misuse Actions

Eduardo B. Fernandez, Michael VanHilst, Maria M. Larrondo Petrie, and
Shihong Huang
Department of Computer Science & Engineering
Florida Atlantic University
777 Glades Road, SE-300, Boca Raton, Florida 33431-0991 USA
{ed, mike, maria, shihong}@cse.fau.edu
URL: http://www.cse.fau.edu/~security

Abstract. An important aspect of security requirements is the understanding and listing of the possible threats to the system. Only then can we decide what specific defense mechanisms to use. We show here an approach to list all threats by considering each action in each use case and analyzing how it can be subverted by an internal or external attacker. From this list we can deduce what policies are necessary to prevent or mitigate the threats. These policies can then be used as guidelines for design. The proposed method can include formal design notations for validation and verification.

1 Introduction

Defining security requirements is difficult and there is no generally accepted way [1], [2], [3], [4], [5]. An important aspect of security requirements is the listing of the possible threats to the system. Only then can we decide what specific defense mechanisms to use. A threat is a potential attack, while an attack is an actual misuse of information. Most approaches consider only the effect of low-level attacks; e.g., taking control of the database system through a buffer overflow attack. There are two problems with this approach: the number of such threats is very high, and we need to make assumptions about a system that has not yet been built. A way to avoid the first problem is the use of sets of generic attacks [6], but this approach cannot avoid the second drawback.

We believe that we should look at the higher levels of the system. An attacker has an objective or goal that he wants to accomplish, e.g., steal the identity of a customer, transfer money to his own account, etc. Security requirements should

Please use the following format when citing this chapter:

Fernández, E.B., VanHilst, M., Petrie, M.M.L., Huang, S., 2006, in IFIP International Federation for Information Processing, Volume 219, Advanced Software Engineering: Expanding the Frontiers of Software Technology, eds. Ochoa, S., Roman, G.-C., (Boston: Springer), pp. 123–137.

define the needs of the system without committing to specific mechanisms. We show here an approach to list threats by considering each action in each use case and seeing how it can be subverted by an internal or external attacker. We assume that the functional use cases have already been defined or are being defined concurrently. From the list of threats we can deduce what policies are necessary to prevent or mitigate the attacks. The proposed method is extendable to include formal design notations for validation and verification; we explore some possibilities. While there is no guarantee that our approach produces all possible threats, it appears superior to other approaches with similar objectives.

A related approach is the concept of misuse cases [1], [7]. Misuse cases are independent use cases initiated by external attackers to the system. That approach, by itself, lacks completeness because it is not clear what misuse cases should be considered. Another related approach is risk analysis. In risk analysis, threats to the successful completion and use of the system are identified and analyzed. Threat likelihood and consequences are considered in a cost benefit analysis, and plans are made to address them. Risk analysis, per se, lacks a method of systematically identifying the threats, it concentrates on the effect of threats on the system.

In previous work we introduced a methodology for secure systems design that uses architectural layers and security patterns [8], [9]. An important aspect of that methodology is the emphasis on approaching security at all stages. The approach presented here would be one of the first stages in using that methodology.

Section 2 discusses some background on use cases. Section 3 presents the concept of misuse actions and shows through an example of how to relate threats to use cases. Section 4 shows how we can define policies to prevent the identified attacks. Section 5 compares our approach to other approaches. The paper ends with some conclusions.

2   Use cases, threats, and policies

Use cases are interactions of a user with the system [10]. The set of all use cases is described by a UML Use Case diagram. Each use case is described by a textual template identifying actors (or stakeholders), preconditions, postconditions, normal flow of execution, and alternate flows of execution. Sequence diagrams may complement the textual descriptions. Use cases are not atomic but consist of a sequence of actions. For example, in a use case to borrow a book from the library one must check if the user has a valid account (first action), she is not overdue (second action), the copy of the book is set to not available (third action), etc. Complex use cases may have many actions. Since use cases identify the actor that performs the use case, we can also identify who is the possible attacker.

As indicated earlier, an attacker has an objective or goal that he wants to accomplish. To accomplish his purposes, he must interact with the system trying to subvert one or more actions in a use case (he might do this indirectly). Low level actions, such as attacking a system through a buffer overflow, are just ways to accomplish these goals but not goals in themselves. Looking at use cases is consistent with the idea that security must be defined at the highest system levels, a basic principle for secure systems [11].

There is a large variety of possible security policies and it is not clear in general, which ones are needed in a given system. Once we understand the possible threats, we can define policies to stop them. These policies are used in turn to guide the selection and implementation of security mechanisms; for example where in the system we should use authentication and the type of authentication required. If the threats indicate that we require authorization we can then find the specific authorization rules that are needed. In an earlier paper we proposed a way to find all the rights needed by the actors of a set of use cases in an application [12]. The idea is that all the use cases of an application define all the possible interactions of actors with the application. We need to provide these actors with rights to perform their functions. If we give these actors only those rights, we are applying the basic principle of least privilege. If we define appropriate rights, attacks can be prevented or mitigated.

3 Threats and actions

We illustrate our approach through an example. Consider a financial company that provides investment services to its customers. Customers can open and close accounts in person or through the Internet. Customers who hold accounts can send orders to the company for buying or selling commodities (stocks, bonds, real estate, art, etc.). Each customer account is in the charge of a custodian (a broker), who carries out the orders of the customers. Customers send orders to their brokers by email or by phone. A government auditor visits periodically to check for application of laws and regulations. Figure 1 shows the Use Case diagram for this institution.

Figure 2 shows the activity diagram for the use case "Open account" in this institution, indicating the typical actions required to open an account for a new customer. We indicate "swimlanes" for Customer and Manager, the two actors involved in this use case [13]. These actions result in new information, including objects for the new customer, her account, and her card-based authorization.

Potentially each action (activity) is susceptible to attack, although not necessarily through the computer system. Figure 3 shows the same activity diagram showing possible threats and including a new swimlane for an external attacker. For this use case we could have the following threats:

- A1. The customer is an impostor and opens an account in the name of another person
- A2. The customer provides false information and opens an spurious account
- A3. The manager is an impostor and collects data illegally
- A4. The manager collects customer information to use illegally
- A5. The manager creates a spurious account with the customer's information
- A6. The manager creates a spurious authorization card to access the account
- A7. An attacker tries to prevent the customers to access their accounts (denial of service)
- A8. An attacker tries to move money from an account to her own account

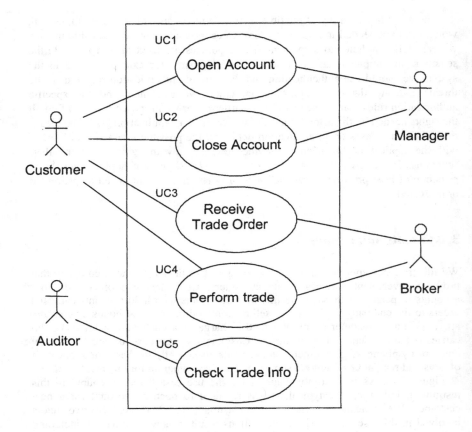

Fig. 1. Use cases for a financial institution

In the activity diagram in Figure 3 the attacks are shown as misuse actions (dotted lines). Undesired consequences in the form of additional or alternative objects (dotted lines) have also been added. With these annotations, the attacks and vulnerabilities presented by the use case become part of our understanding of the use case and are explicit in its analysis.

Note that:

- We can identify internal and external attackers. The actors in these attacks could be external attackers (hackers), acting as such or hackers impersonating legitimate roles. It is also possible that a person in a legitimate role can be malicious (internal attacks). For example, A1 and A3 are performed by external attackers; A2, A4, A5 and A6 are performed by insiders, while A7 and A8 are performed by either external or internal attackers.

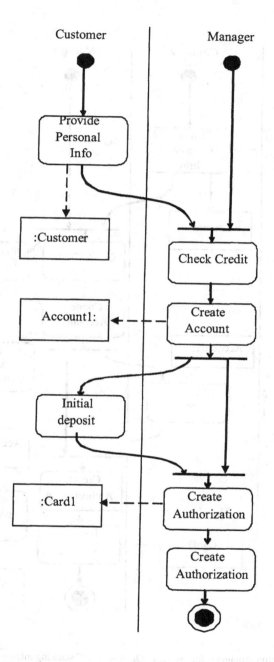

Fig. 2. Activity diagram for use case "Open account"

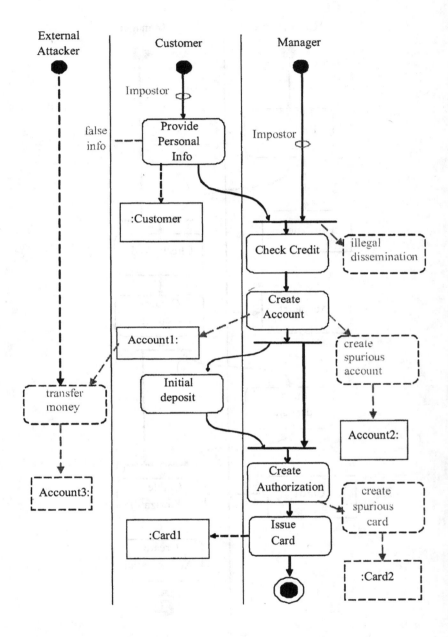

Fig. 3. Activity diagram for use case "Open account" showing misuse actions

- We can list systematically all (or most) possible application threats. While completeness cannot be assured, the fact that we consider all actions in a use case gives us some confidence that we considered at least all important possible attacks. The threats that we postulate come from our experience, from the knowledge of the application, and from the study of similar systems (banking systems have similar threats).
- We can later identify the target of the low-level attacks. Starting from the threats to actions we can look at the lower levels of the systems already designed and search for possible realizations of the threats, e.g. a buffer overflow, bypassing entry points of a procedure, etc.
- Note that we only consider attacks to our system. Attacks to systems that collaborate with our system are beyond our control. For example, credit checking is normally performed using an external service. If that service was compromised we could receive erroneous information about a potential customer and make a wrong decision about his account.
- We are not restricted to analyze each use case in isolation. Some workflows require several use cases, e.g. "Approve a purchase order" can be followed by "Send a purchase order". We can consider attacks that take advantages of this sequence, for example, by bypassing some steps that perform checks. These threats, in general, are harder to find.
- The sequence used in the example to open an account in a financial institution is very similar to opening an account in a bank, in a club, or in a library. In fact, we can think of it as a pattern and it could be an addition to a pattern for building the corresponding software [14]. Having threat patterns simplifies finding threats for new systems.

4 Stopping or mitigating the attacks

We can now find out what policies are needed to stop these attacks. For this purpose, we can select from the typical policies used in secure systems [11]. This selection should result in a minimum set of mechanisms instead of mechanisms piled up because they might be useful. For example, to avoid impostors we can have a policy of I&A (Identification and Authentication) for every actor participating in a use case.

To stop or mitigate the attacks in the example we need the following policies:

- A1. A3. Mutual authentication. Every interaction across system nodes is authenticated.
- A2. Verify source of information.
- A4. Logging. Since the manager is using his legitimate rights we can only log his actions for auditing at a later time.
- A5. A6. Separation of administration from use of data. For example, a manager can create accounts but should have no rights to withdraw or deposit money in the account.
- A7. Protection against denial of service. We need some redundancy in the system to increase its availability. Intrusion detection and filtering policies should also be useful.

- A8. Authorization. If the user is not explicitly authorized he should not be able to move money from any account.

  The lower levels of the system should enforce these policies. If they are properly designed we do not need to identify every low-level threat.

5   Formalization

The analysis of attacks and their prevention can be formalized as shown in Figure 4. The preconditions for undesired consequences are presented in comments. For the analysis we focus only on sufficient preconditions that should not normally be present at that point in the execution of the use case. In some cases the preconditions are simple conjunctions, where all conditions must be present. In other cases, the preconditions may involve more complicated logical relationships among preconditions.

To express relationships among preconditions, we have adopted the concise notation from RSML [15]. Preconditions are represented in tabular form as disjunctions of conjunctions (disjunctive normal form). Each column in the table is a sufficient set of preconditions. Within each column, the role of a precondition literal (True, False, or don't care) is given by the letters T, F, or X. For example, a spurious account could be created either when a malicious manager acts without customer approval, or when there is an error (intended or unintended) in the customer information.

Figure 5 shows the equivalent fault tree representation for one set of preconditions. A fault tree analysis allows probabilities of occurrence to be estimated for each condition or event. The fault tree can be expanded, with sub-dependencies, to assist in this process. In a fault tree a circle or ellipse represents a basic condition, while a diamond represents a condition that could be further elaborated. An error in the customer info is treated as basic – it doesn't matter how or why the error was made. Customer approval could be further expanded, for example to show an "or" condition between customer signing an acknowledgement or customer receiving notification. Similarly, alternative preconditions for a malicious person acting in the role of manager could be explored.

In analyzing risks and their prevention, it is important to make a distinction between the actual desired condition, and the mechanism that is used to achieve it. For example, a good manager is a desired condition for secure transactions. Authorization is a mechanism to reduce the likelihood of a bad manager being able to accomplish his purposes. But authorization is, itself, not the desired goal, and may, in fact, be neither sufficient nor the only means of achieving the goal condition. In this sense, our analysis approach is consistent with the spirit of goal oriented practices [2, 16].

In the formalized analysis, the defense policies and mechanisms must be shown to reduce the probability of each sufficient set of preconditions to an acceptable level of risk. An actual formal analysis is beyond the scope of the present paper. However, we can give a sense of how such analyses could be performed using fault tree and model checking techniques.

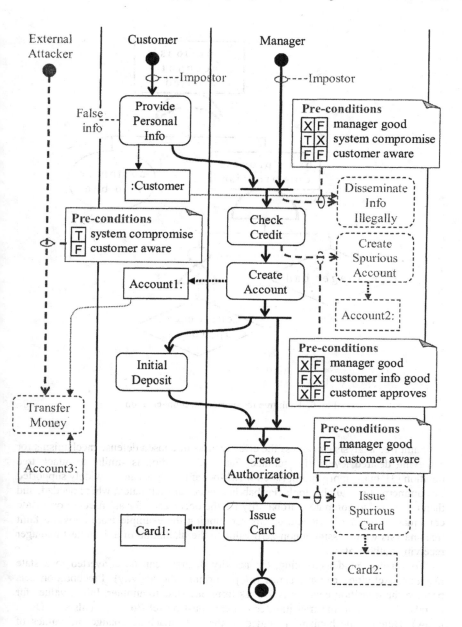

Fig. 4. Formalizing the analysis of attacks and preventions

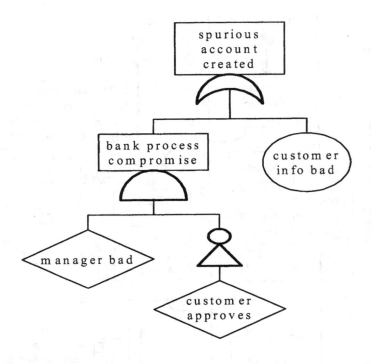

Fig. 5. Fault tree for spurious account creation

Fault tree analysis can assess the effectiveness of chosen defense mechanisms for achieving desired levels of assurance. Fault tree notation is similar to attack tree notation [3], but is more appropriate for risk-benefit analyses and is widely supported by commercially available tools. Probability values are estimated, where needed, and then combined to compute a probability for the occurrence for an insecure or unsafe combination of conditions and events. Continuing the example from above, a fault tree analysis would assign a non-zero value to the likelihood of a dishonest manager receiving authorization.

To perform model checking, the activity diagram can be converted to a state machine. Activities become states (of performing the activity). Precondition sets become the transition conditions to pass from one state to another. Initial values for literals appearing in the transition conditions must be set (to True, False, or Don't know). Defense mechanisms included in the state machine change the values of literals when visited.

6   Discussion

The closest approach to ours is clearly the one based on misuse cases [1], [7]. Misuse cases are not developed systematically and it is easy to miss important attacks. That approach also uses other use cases to mitigate or prevent attacks. Use cases are interactions of users with the system but attack prevention cannot be done in general through additional interactions. We need instead security policies and the corresponding mechanisms to implement them. Misuse cases because of their reliance on whole use cases they need to define new stereotypes such as "threaten" and "mitigate" use cases, while we just use standard use cases. We do not think that the emphasis on protecting assets is also the best for information systems. Emphasis on assets makes sense when we are talking of physical assets that can be stolen. Information security is about preventing illegal reading or modification of information as well as assuring its availability. It makes then more sense to defend against specific actions, e.g. stealing identity, instead of protecting the identity database.

The group at the Open University in the U.K. has done a significant amount of work on security requirements [17], including the use of abuse frames to lead to security requirements (an abuse frame is similar to a misuse case but using Jackson's problem frames [18].

[2] discusses requirements for secure systems using the concept of goal-oriented requirements. Other authors also have focused on security requirements [5], [19] but none of them consider use cases. Mouratidis and his group use a special methodology, Tropos, to model security. Their approach to develop requirements does not consider use cases either [20].

Van Lamsweerde considers anti-models, which describe how specifications of model elements could be maliciously threatened, why and by whom [21]. His approach combines ideas from misuse cases and goal-oriented requirements.

All these models consider a coarser unit that can be attacked and are less systematic than our approach.

7   A methodology to build secure systems

This work is part of a methodology to build secure systems. Of course, it does not need to be applied as part of this approach but the methodology provides a context for our development. A main idea in the proposed methodology is that security principles should be applied at every stage of the software lifecycle and that each stage can be tested for compliance with security principles. Another basic idea is the use of patterns to guide security at each stage [9]. Figure 6 shows a secure software lifecycle, indicating where security can be applied (white arrows) and where we can audit for compliance with security principles and policies (dark arrows).

This project proposes guidelines for incorporating security from the requirements stage through analysis, design, implementation, testing, and deployment. Our approach considers the following development stages:

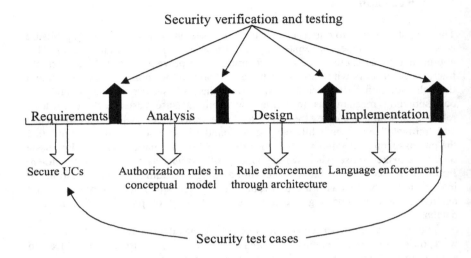

Fig. 6. Secure software lifecycle

Domain analysis stage: A business model is defined.   Legacy systems are identified and their security implications analyzed.   Domain and regulatory constraints are identified.   Policies must be defined up front, in this phase. The suitability of the development team is assessed, possibly leading to added training. Security issues of the developers, themselves, and their environment may also be considered in some cases.   This phase may be performed only once for each new domain or team.

Requirements stage: Use cases define the required interactions with the system. Applying the principle that security must start from the highest levels, it makes sense to relate attacks to use cases. We study each action within a use case and see which threats are possible (this paper).   We then determine which policies would stop these attacks. From the use cases we can also determine the needed rights for each actor and thus apply a need-to-know policy. Note that the set of all use cases defines all the uses of the system and from all the use cases we can determine all the rights for each actor. The security test cases for the complete system are also defined at this stage.

Analysis stage: Analysis patterns can be used to build the conceptual model in a more reliable and efficient way. Security patterns describe security models or mechanisms. We can build a conceptual model where repeated applications of a security model pattern realize the rights determined from use cases. In fact, analysis patterns can be built with predefined authorizations according to the roles in their use cases. Then we only need to additionally specify the rights for those parts not covered by patterns. We can start defining mechanisms (countermeasures) to prevent attacks.

Design stage: Design stage: when we have the possible attacks to a system, design mechanisms are selected to stop these attacks. User interfaces should correspond to use cases and may be used to enforce the authorizations defined in the analysis stage. Secure interfaces enforce authorizations when users interact with the system. Components can be secured by using authorization rules for Java or .NET components. Distribution provides another dimension where security restrictions can be applied. Deployment diagrams can define secure configurations to be used by security administrators. A multilayer architecture is needed to enforce the security constraints defined at the application level. In each level we use patterns to represent appropriate security mechanisms. Security constraints must be mapped between levels.

Implementation stage: This stage requires reflecting in the code the security rules defined in the design stage. Because these rules are expressed as classes, associations, and constraints, they can be implemented as classes in object-oriented languages. In this stage we can also select specific security packages or COTS, e.g., a firewall product, a cryptographic package. Some of the patterns identified earlier in the cycle can be replaced by COTS (these can be tested to see if they include a similar pattern).

7   Conclusions

We have presented an approach that produces all (or most) of the threats to a given application. This happens because we consider systematically all actions within a use case and we see how they could be subverted. While all this could be done in the textual version of the use case, the use of UML activity diagrams produces a clear and more intuitive way to analyze these attacks. From the threats we derive necessary policies to stop or mitigate them.

We have now completed the requirements stage and we are ready to start defining the solution to our design problem. Each identified threat can be analyzed to see how it can be accomplished in the specific environment. The list can then be used to guide the design and to select security products. It can also be used to evaluate the final design by analyzing whether the system defenses can stop all these attacks. As we indicated earlier since use cases define all the interactions with the system we can find from them the rights needed by these roles to perform their work (need to know). Future work will concentrate in the transition from the policies to the mechanisms.

When dealing with a complex safety-critical software system, the number and complexity of threats will increase; for example, there may be more than one way to attack a particular action. Without proper mechanisms to represent this information, software developers will have difficulty to effectively digest the information and to validate the design and implementation. Another future work is to find a better way, considering layout, style etc, to document the misuse action diagrams, that can be effective even for complex systems. Some work has been done to assess the efficacy of UML diagrams as one type of graphical documentation [22], [23]. For example, we can use annotated UML activity diagrams and Interaction Overview Diagrams to assess the best way to document misuse actions, according to quality attributes such as completeness and effectiveness.

Acknowledgements

The referees made useful comments that improved this paper. This work was supported by a grant from the US Department of Information Security Agency (DISA), administered by Pragmatics, Inc.

References

1. Alexander, I.: Misuse cases: Use cases with hostile intent. In *IEEE Software*, Vol. 20, No. 1, January/February 2003, IEEE Computer Society Press, Los Alamitos, California (2003) 58-66.
2. Liu, L., Yu, E. and Mylopoulos, J.: Security and privacy requirements analysis within a social setting. In *Proceedings of the 11th IEEE International Conference on Requirements Engineering (RE'03)*, Monterey, California, 8-12 September 2003, IEEE Computer Society Press, Los Alamitos, California (2003) 151-161.
3. Schneier, B.: Attack Trees: Modeling Security Threats. In *Dr. Dobb's Journal*, Vol. 24, No. 12, December 1999, CMP Media LLC., Manhasset, New York, USA (2003) 21-29.
4. Whitmore, . J. J.: A method for designing secure solutions. In *IBM Systems Journal*, Vol. 40, No. 3, IBM, Riverton, New Jersey, USA (2001) 747-768. http://www.research.ibm.com/journal/sj
5. Zuccato, A.: Holistic security requirement engineering for electronic commerce. In *Computers & Security*, Vol. 23, No. 1, Elsevier, UK (2004) 63-76.
6. Howard, M., and LeBlanc, D. *Writing secure code*, (2nd Ed.), Microsoft Press, Redmond, Washington, USA (2003).
7. Sindre, G. and Opdahl, A.L.: Eliciting Security Requirements by Misuse Cases. In *Proceedings of the 37th International Conference on Technology of Object-Oriented Languages and Systems* (TOOLS-Pacific 2000), Sydney, Australia, 20-23 November 2000 IEEE Press, Los Alamitos, California, USA (2000) 120 –131.
8. Fernandez, E. B.: A methodology for secure software design. In *Software Engineering Research and Practice: Proceedings of the International Conference on Software Engineering Research and Practice*, SERP '04, Las Vegas, Nevada, USA, Vol. 1, 21-24 June 2004, H. R. Arabnia and H. Reza (eds.), CSREA Press, USA (2004) 130-136.
9 Fernandez, E. B., Larrondo-Petrie, M. M., Sorgente, T. and VanHilst M.: A methodology to develop secure systems using patterns. In *Integrating security and software engineering: Advances and future vision*, H. Mouratidis and P. Giorgini (Eds.), Idea Group, Hershey, Pennsylvania, USA (2006).
10. Larman, C.: *Applying UML and Patterns: An Introduction to Object-Oriented Analysis and Design and Iterative Development* (3rd edition.), Prentice-Hall, Englewood Cliffs, New Jersey, USA (2005).
11. Fernandez, E. B., Gudes, E. and Olivier, M.: *The Design of Secure Systems*, Addison-Wesley, Reading, Massachussetts, USA (2007).
12 Fernandez, E. B., and Hawkins, J.C.: Determining Role Rights from Use Cases. In *Proceedings of the 2nd ACM Workshop on Role-Based Access Control*, RBAC'97, Fairfax, Virginia, USA, 6-7 November 1997, ACM Press, New York, New York, USA (1997) 121-125.
13. Booch, G., Rumbaugh, J. and Jacobson, I.: *The Unified Modeling Language User Guide* (2nd Ed.), Addison-Wesley, Upper Saddle River, New Jersey, USA (2005).
14. Fernandez, E. B. and Liu, Y.: The Account Analysis Pattern. In *Proceedings of EuroPLoP 2002 (Pattern Languages of Programs)*, Irsee Germany, 3-7 July 2002, Universitätsverlag Konstanz, Konstanz, Germany, (2002). http://www.hillside.net/patterns/EuroPLoP2002/

15. Leveson, N. G., Heimdahl, M. P. E., Hildreth, H. and Reese, J. D.: Requirements specification for process control systems. In *IEEE Transactions on Software Engineering,* Vol. 20, No 9, September 1994, IEEE Computer Society Press, Los Alamitos, California, USA (1994) 684-707.
16. Cleland-Huang, J., Denne, M., Mahjub, G., and Patel, N.: A goal-oriented approach for mitigating security and continuity risks. In *Proceedings. of the IEEE Inernational. Symposium on Secure Software Engineering (ISSSE'06),*13-15 March 2006, Arlington, Virginia, USA (2006) 167-177.
17. Haley, C.B., Laney, R.C., and Nuseiben, B.: Deriving security requirements from crosscutting threat descriptions. In *Proceedings of the 3rd. International Conference on Aspect-Oriented Software Development (AOSD'04),* Lancaster, UK, 22-26 March 2004, ACM Press, New York, New York, USA (2004) 112-121.
18. Jackson, M.: Problem *Frames: Analysing and structuring software development problems*, Addison-Wesley, Reading, Washington, USA (2001).
19. He, Q. and Anton, A. I.: Deriving access control policies from requirements specifications and database design, North Carolina State University CS Technical Report. TR-2004-24, (2004).
20. Mouratidis, H.,Giorgini, P. and Manson, G.A.: Using security attach scenarios to analyse security during information systems Design. In *Proceedings of the 2nd International Workshop on Security in Information Systems at ICEIS 2004,* Porto, Portugal, April 2004 (2004) 10-17.
21. van Lamsweerde, A.: Elaborating security requirements by construction of intentional anti-models. In *Proceedings of the 26th International Conference on Software Engineering* (ICSE'04), Edinburgh, UK, 23-28 May 2004, IEEE Computer Society Press, Los Alamitos, California, USA (2004)148-157.
22. Huang, S. and Tilley, A.: Workshop on Graphical Documentation for Programmers: Assessing the Efficacy of UML Diagrams for Program Understanding. Held in conjunction with *The 11th International Workshop on Program Comprehension,* IWPC 2003, 10 May 2003, Portland, Oregon, USA, IEEE Computer Society Press, Los Alamitos, California, USA (2003) 281-282.
23. Tilley, S., and Huang, S.: A qualitative assessment of the efficacy of UML diagrams as a form of graphical documentation in aiding program understanding. In *Proceedings of the 21st ACM Annual International Conference on Design of Communication* (SIGDOC 2003: 12-15 October 2003; San Francisco, California, USA, ACM Press: New York, New York, USA (2003) 184-191.

Experiences in Portable Mobile Application Development

Antti Kantee and Heikki Vuolteenaho

Helsinki University of Technology

Abstract. In the software world portability means power. The more operating environments you can support out of the same code tree means more potential users for your software. If done right, additional platforms can be supported with little extra maintenance cost. If done wrong, maintaining additional platforms will become a veritable nightmare.

This paper describes experiences undergone when creating truly portable software. Our software is a real time rendered 3D map and messaging application, which runs on UNIX (Linux, Mac OS X, NetBSD), Windows 98/2000/XP, Windows CE and Symbian Series 60. It is Symbian which makes this mix of platforms interesting and challenging. However, with the knowledge of potential problems, we found that this set of platforms is totally manageable for a portable mobile 3D application.

1 Introduction

Traditionally, in the UNIX and C world, portability has come to stand for the ability of a software to deal with differences imposed by the underlying CPU architecture, such as byte order, pointer size or alignment constraints [4, 5]. Other usual suspects for hindering a porting process are standard library or system interfaces either missing or behaving differently. By carefully programming against POSIX and ISO C provided interfaces and avoiding making assumptions about the compiler or underlying hardware, it is possible to achieve a fairly high level of portability, even between UNIX and Windows.

However, when a completely different kind of system, Symbian, is introduced into the picture, the rules change. All assumptions which used to hold in the UNIX and Windows environments may no longer be valid. This does not necessarily make things more complex or difficult. The major factor of difficulties for having Symbian within the sphere of portability of a software is basing key design elements on non-valid assumptions.

This paper describes the issues encountered in developing a mobile 3D application written in C. In Chapter 2 we describe issues specific to Symbian while Chapter 3 concentrates on issues affecting all platforms.

Please use the following format when citing this chapter:

Kantee, A., Vuolteenaho, H., 2006, in IFIP International Federation for Information Processing, Volume 219, Advanced Software Engineering: Expanding the Frontiers of Software Technology, eds. Ochoa, S., Roman, G.-C., (Boston: Springer), pp. 138–152.

1.1 The software: mLOMA

mLOMA [13] (mobile LOcation aware Messaging Application) is in its essence a 3D map application optimized for mobile devices and built on top of OpenGL [9]and GLUT [6]. The mLOMA client can be used to browse a real time rendered 3D scene with a framerate acceptable for interactive use. It features a route guidance system and support for GPS location tracking. A server component is also provided. If a network connection is available, clients can receive up-to-date information on the model and interact using the server. Users can track each others' locations and communicate using messages. Messages can be public or targeted to individual users and they can be attached to any points in space or the model.

Fig. 1. mLOMA client running on Pocket PC and Symbian Series 60 platforms

Since mobile terminals do not feature 3D acceleration in hardware and are limited both in terms of available CPU power and memory, the implementation must try to limit resource consumption to a minimum. This is in part done by doing a PVS precalculation on the 3D scene [13] and the rest is accomplished by non-wasteful C programming.

1.2 Portability

For defining portability, we first separate the whole idea of portability into two different categories: code portability and concept portability. Concept portability refers to the ability to implement an idea on a variety of platforms. For example, a user interface requiring a cursor is not completely portable to all mobile computing platforms, since some platforms lack a pointer device. On those platforms it is possible to emulate a pointer device, but this will affect usability and is therefore visible to the end user.

Code portability is the ability of software to run common lines of code between the various platforms it is portable to. The code lines which cannot be shared result from differences in the various platforms either in system interfaces or from the hardware. Code portability involves crafting interfaces which abstract the underlying platform functionality where it is different. Abstracing does, however, come with a price of call indirection and increased coding effort, and therefore should be carried out only where necessary. We use the term *machine independent* (MI) to describe code which runs on all platforms and the term *machine dependent* (MD) to describe code which runs only on a certain platform. Software with code portability will have a high MI/MD ratio in terms of lines of code.

Implementing a certain functionality multiple times for different platforms when not really necessary is in its essence confusing code portability with concept portability. The resulting user-perceived functionality will be the same, but the cost of maintaining several different implementations is much higher and will probably lead to broken platforms as code evolves [7, 11]. It is easy to see why, since as the number of lines of code shared between platforms goes down, the portion of the codebase that can be tested on a single platforms goes down as well.

1.3 Symbian

Symbian is an operating system designed primarily for mobile phones and other mobile devices. Conserving limited resources is a priority, and several programming practices used on Symbian encourage it. This makes working with Symbian in a multi-platform project a challenging task.

While fully understanding Symbian requires closer attention, this paper does not cover the architecture of Symbian and such studies can be found in dedicated literature [3, 17].

2 Porting to Symbian

The mLOMA client was originally written for Linux desktops, Windows desktops and Windows CE PDA devices. Symbian Series 60 support was not originally planned. However, once capable mobile terminals became available, support was required.

2.1 GLUT

Symbian lacks a platform-provided GLUT [6] implementation. GLUT, tersely put, works as an event handler in between the application and console (windowing, input devices). Generally, implementations never come out of the main event loop until they detect the quit command being issued. However, due to the active object scheduling scheme used in Symbian applications [12], we cannot run continuosly in the main loop. Instead, we need to periodically relinquish control of execution and generate events to regain control.

A subset implementation of GLUT for Windows CE had been done earlier in the project, since GLUT was not available for it at that time [1]. However, this implementation is mostly incompatible with the Symbian programming restrictions and in addition was built on top of the normal application-transparent preemptive scheduling principle.

We ended up with two separate GLUT implementations. While this is in disagreement with our portability rule set forth in Chapter 1.2, it is important to note this as an acceptable and even encouraged exception to the rule. First of all, code lines are not shared because there are not very many lines to share: approximately 415 of the total 496 lines in the implementation are completely specific to Symbian. Second, the GLUT interface is very unlikely to change and therefore require platform-specific maintenance.

2.2 Writable global data in DLLs

Symbian GUI applications are built as DLLs and Symbian does not allow writable global data in DLLs [3]. There are two choices: build an EXE instead of a DLL or get rid of all global writable data. The first option makes building a traditional Symbian GUI very complicated [21].

Each thread can store exactly one word of global writable data in a slot called Thread Local Storage (TLS). We put all our global variables inside a (rather large) struct and push the struct pointer to TLS. Accessing the TLS is slower than a regular function call, in our testing it was roughly 20 times slower. Because of this, we often pass the pointer as an extra parameter in often-used function calls. However, we noticed that passing "a pointer to globals" was detrimental for the interface development within the client. Especially junior programmers had the habit of crafting interfaces with nothing but that pointer passed.

Symbian tools are not helpful in locating global writable data in the program, as they do not even specify the offending module:

```
ERROR: Dll 'MLOMA[102048D8].APP'
  has uninitialised data.
```

Symbian developers have found ways to extract the offending source modules and variables [18], but they are not very practical. A much better way of locating

---

[1] However, GLUT|ES is now available for Windows CE.

modules and code fragments in violation of this restriction is to use a typical UNIX command sequence:

```
find . -name \*.o                       \
   | xargs nm -o --defined-only          \
   | awk '$2 !~ /[tTrR]/{print $0}'
```

If the filter encounters a symbol type that is not *text* or *read-only data*, it prints the module and symbol name. After this, it is easy to use a text editor to search for the culprit symbol in the offending module.

Notice, that for this to work, nm must support the object format of the objects it is supposed to examine. It is most natural to run this on a UNIX development platform against UNIX objects, although it should be possible to use a UNIX-hosted toolchain, such as the one provided by the GNUPoc project, for running it against Symbian object files.

2.3 Stack size

In C programming it is customary to allocate memory for local operations from the current stack frame, from where it will be automatically freed when upon return. In most environments it is safe to assume at least tens or hundreds of kilobytes of stack space, making allocating fairly large objects from the stack possible.

Symbian has a comparatively small default stack size (8kB). Large allocations from stack are therefore impossible. On the device, running out of stack will lead to a crash, but the emulator build fails on purpose if it runs into a dangerously large (>4kB according to our tests) stack frame [2]:

```
MAIN.obj : error LNK2001:
   unresolved external symbol __chkstk
```

To remedy this problem, all large allocations had to be moved from the stack to the heap. It involved some code restructuring, but was mechanical work.

2.4 Texture loading

The mLOMA client needs to load JPEG and PNG images to show textures on the 3D map. On platforms other than Symbian the open source libraries libjpeg and libpng are used for this purpose. However, these libraries have not been ported to Symbian. Porting them is problematic at best because of the writable global data limitation discussed in Chapter 2.2. Symbian does have a native API for image loading and we use that instead.

The Symbian image loading APIs are asynchronous (non-blocking), while on the other platforms they are synchronous (blocking); the client was designed

---

[2] Notice that running out of stack is still possible in case of a deep enough call recursion without any single stack frames running over the warning limit.

fairly heavily on synchronous interfaces meaning that it expects the image to loaded once the image loading call returns. We used a nested active scheduler loop to effectively make the loading process appear synchronous [1], although this is strongly discouraged [16]. We ran into several problematic situations because of this. Normally application code handling an event runs without interruption (non-preemptively). But while the image loading function is blocking (using nested scheduling), the nested scheduler is free to schedule other active objects requiring attention. This causes for example reentrancy problems, as we enter GLUT through the active scheduler (Chapter 2.1). Several workarounds were introduced into the code, but, needless to say, these problems were extremely difficult to locate and the resulting bug symptoms may occur only in rare corner cases.

One possibility would have been to convert the entire application to deal with asynchronous interfaces. This, however, would have been poor choice unless the previously synchronous image loading backends would have been converted to asynchronous also. The reason is that different behaviour would have introduced platform specific bugs. Converting the sychronous backends to asychronous would have meant introducing threads into the program. The authors generally consider threading to be harmful [20]. Specific to this case, we probably would have run across different platforms exhibiting different threading behaviour.

A better solution to the problem came from an isolation technique [14] used, amongst other locations, in the popular OpenSSH networking daemon. In MD Symbian startup we create a thread whose only function is to handle texture loading. Communication between the application execution context and texture thread happens through a synchronization primitive. The application first triggers the texture loading and then sleeps on top of the synchronization primitive. When texture loading is complete, the texture thread triggers the application to continue executing. After replacing the nested scheduler with this scheme, all inexplicable crashes disappeared. We propose that all who want to emulate sychronous interfaces on Symbian use this method.

2.5 Stdio problems with locales

The stdio call families of `printf` and `scanf()` have a problem with the thousands separator and decimal separator on Symbian. It seems that modifying the application's private locale does not affect the separators at all and using the system-wide locale it is only possible to change the characters, not totally remove them (more important for the thousands separator). This leads to a situation where it is not possible to reliably read and write floating point numbers from using an externally provided source, such as a config file.

Third party options were not available due to licensing or problems with globals (see Chapter 2.2), so we crafted our own implementations called `fgetfloat()` and `fputfloat()`, which read and write, respectively, a float using the given stdio stream. These are suboptimal, because they disrupt code flow.

In retrospect, the right choice would have been to drop floating points from files all together.

3 Problems & solutions, tools

3.1 The build process

Currently, using the native build systems for each platform, we have different build systems for:

- UNIX desktops: Linux, Mac OS X, NetBSD (make & GNU'ish toolchain)
- Windows (MS Developer Studio, Visual C++)
- Windows CE, PocketPC 2002 (MS Developer Studio, Visual C++)
- Windows CE, PocketPC 2003 (MS Developer Studio, Visual C++)
- Symbian Series60 V1 (makmake, Visual C++/gcc)
- Symbian Series60 V2 (makmake, Visual C++/gcc)

This means that adding a source file to the project or for example adding a project-wide C preprocessor definition requires modifying seven different files. The MS Developer Studio projects are not even meant for hand-editing, so touching them from outside the actual IDE is dubious practice.

As the number of platforms increases, the maintenance overhead grows soon beyond acceptable limits. If various platforms require a lot of manual editing to keep up, they will likely end up being out-of-sync with the main development environment. At one point after a project has grown onto multiple platforms, an attempt to unify the build procedures for all platforms should be made.

We will attempt to make this unification for mLOMA in the future. One possibility is to autogenerate the Symbian makmake project files from the UNIX Makefiles and use GNU Make in the Windows builds. The latter is accomplished by a well-known scheme of having a MS Developer Studio project file, which just contains the instructions to run GNU Make for building the project and leaves the details of the build process up to the Makefile.

Another possibility for accomplishing the same effect would be to autogenerate the project files. The UNIX Makefiles could easily be used to act as the autogeneration facility, since they are written in a clean fashion separating input data (e.g. source file names) from rules (e.g. how to product an executable). It should be fairly simple to autogenerate the .mmp files for Symbian builds and there is evidence that autogenerating MS Developer Studio project files is possible [8], even if not directly available.

In a sense, the build system can be equated with program source code and the concept discussed in Chapter 1.2. A portable program will also have a portable and flexible build system.

3.2 Local language support

The mLOMA client application needs to support various different languages, as it is aimed primarily for tourists, who benefit from local-language support. This means that our software cannot include hardcoded messages to the user in the middle of code, but rather the code must contain identifiers, which can be translated on the fly. While is it well-known how to accomplish this on any given platform, for example Linux [2], the problem is finding something usable on all platforms; for example even UNIX vendors cannot agree amongst themselves on should they use catgets() or gettext().

Message database The problem here is not so much abstracting the programming interface as it is abstracting the message database. If we were to use the native i18n services of each platform, it would require us to input the translated messages into several different databases. This would, first of all, mean learning the tools of the various message catalogs. Second, and worse, this would most likely mean that some of the catalogues would be out-of-sync with others, as development takes place on different platforms.

Since we only need to do simple key-to-text translation, a self-authored component was created for translation purposes. This was done by writing a script in *awk* for translating the input text into lookup tables which could be used from within the code. A selection of the input text format is presented in Table 1. This table is translated by the script into code usable at runtime. For all except Symbian, this means creating tables of C strings and for Symbian this means creating resource files and appropriate descriptor tables.

Table 1. Selected example translations from master_ui.txt

```
!fi
FORM_ROUTE_FASTEST Nopein reitti
MENU_HELP Ohjeet
!en
FORM_ROUTE_FASTEST Fastest route
MENU_HELP Help
!et
FORM_ROUTE_FASTEST Kiireim tee
MENU_HELP Abi
```

After the translation tables have been built, they are compiled into the client software and can be accessed through a call to a function a bit misleadingly named localize() [3], for example the call localize(UISTR_MENU_HELP) would produce the string "Ohjeet", "Help", or "Abi" depending on if the selected language was Finnish, English or Estonian, respectively.

---

[3] After all, the call only gives a translation of the string. It does not, for example, convert monetary units, dates or thousands separators to local conventions.

Runtime interface and language selection Deciding which translation to use runtime is equally, if not more, difficult than deciding how to do the translation. In a perfect world it would be possible to do this while holding on to two guidelines: changing the language should be similar on all mLOMA platforms and the method for changing the language should be in alignment with the platform's native way of doing runtime language selection.

POSIX does not specify anything about local language support in the locale interface, so we cannot use the `setlocale()` interface for querying the language: LC_MESSAGES would be close, but not being a part of POSIX it is not defined by Windows. Environment variables (`getenv("LANG")`), are not supported by Windows CE. Symbian has its own framework.

Currently all platforms use specific implementations: UNIX and Windows use `getenv()`, Windows CE uses a compile-time selector and Symbian uses its own resource file framework, which allows the application to select the correct locale at application startup. The future is undecided, although all things considered, a configuration file entry might be the simplest choice even though it means going against established platform conventions.

3.3 Memory management

Our memory resources are different from modern GUI applications. We have to assume an extremely small amount of available memory, around 5MB in the minimum configuration. In addition, there is no secondary memory on the Symbian and Windows CE platforms, so we need to control memory management ourselves.

Our scheme for dealing with the memory limit is simple: we have a wrapper around malloc, `memory_malloc()` [4], which checks if memory allocation fails, frees all memory available to be free'd and tries to allocate the same amount of memory again. Only if this second allocation fails, the wrapper will return a failure to the caller and the caller must deal with the situation.

For parts of allocated memory it is easy to tell if it is currently in use or not. A lot of memory usage comes from the geometric model and associated textures used to render the 3D scene. This static information is easy to reload if it is later required. In a sense, this type of operation can be compared with a practice used in some operating systems, where the read-only text segment is not paged out to secondary memory. To perform a memory sweep in case of a shortage, we simply walk the list of textures and meshes and free ones which are currently not in the field of view.

Tracking allocated memory Symbian is designed for low-memory environments with long-running applications and tries to encourage proper memory

---

[4] For the diversity of platforms we have, it is much simpler to have a completely different symbol name for the memory allocation function than it is to try insert a wrapper using the same name as the platform malloc and still try to call the platform malloc from within the wrapper.

Table 2. CPP tricks for memory allocator interface

memory.h:

```
#ifdef MEMORY_DEBUG
void *memory_malloc(size_t, unsigned /*magic*/,
                    const char *, const char *, int);
#define memory_malloc(a,b)                          \
        memory_malloc(a,b,MEMORY_DEBUG_MAGIC,       \
        __FUNCTION__,__FILE__,__LINE__)
#else
void *memory_malloc(size_t);
#endif /* MEMORY_DEBUG */
```

memory.c

```
#ifdef MEMORY_DEBUG
#undef memory_malloc
void *omamemory_malloc(size_t);
#else
#define omamemory_malloc memory_malloc
#endif /* MEMORY_DEBUG */
```

management habits to avoid memory leaks. This exhibits itself by the debug builds panicking at exit if any allocated (non-freed) memory remains. Most UNIX and Windows programs do not free their memory upon exit, as keeping track of all memory allocations requires extra work and in any case the operating system will unmap the pages of an exiting process.

While we could simply not care about the issue, as Symbian release builds do not complain, playing along with the platform memory management functionality seems like a correct option. This mandates us to do memory tracking if we wish to avoid two related problems: the Symbian debug builds panicking upon exit and standard desktop programming practices contributing such errors. While a tool such a Valgrind [10]would work perfectly for this, normal development cycles are not usually done within it and since we already feature our own malloc(), coupling tracking with it is the right choice.

Fig. 2. Memory meta information reserved by our malloc()

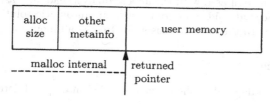

Some `malloc()` implementations register the amount of memory reserved in extra space right before the pointer returned to the caller [19], also illustrated in Figure 2. Our idea is to use this same space to achieve an $O(1)$ lookup for memory allocation chunk describing metadata. Using the information contained in the chunks of metadata, the application prints out diagnostic messages when exiting:

```
non-free'd chunk at 0x8a16a1c, size 0x24
main/mother.c:mother_init(), line 55
```

This indicates that memory reserved from the module mother.c, in the function `mother_init()`, on line 55 in the module was not freed before exit. Upon seeing this message, it is much easier to figure out what is going wrong than from having the program crash on the Symbian platform with the following error message:

```
Program closed: MLOMA ALLOC: 132df248 0
```

By using certain C preprocessor tricks illustrated in Table 2, memory allocation works, without any modifications to calling code, for the memory wrappers compiled with or without `MEMORY_DEBUG` and the calling code compiled with or without `MEMORY_DEBUG`. The tracking layer is implemented directly as `memory_malloc` and it calls the backend called `omamemory_malloc`. If the memory module is compiled without `MEMORY_DEBUG`, the call to the tracking layer is simply skipped by renaming the `omamemory_malloc` symbol. In the opposite case, a caller compiled without `MEMORY_DEBUG` will not pass the correct `MEMORY_DEBUG_MAGIC` signalling that the rest of the arguments are garbage and should not be examined.

Table 3. Compiled (gcc 3.3.3, NetBSD/i386) total size of memory free'ing subroutines

optimization flags	resulting code size (bytes)
-O0	2485
-O2	1770
-Os	1534

We could of course use the metainformation to free all memory, but it was decided against that. First of all, the code size (Table 3) for the freeing code is insignificant when compared with the allocation overhead, at least two pointers per allocation. Second, and more important, an automatic solution would not be in alignment with the original reason for freeing all memory.

3.4 Networking

The networking code used in the client is divided into four different layers.

1. platform-provided networking interface

2. platform-specific implementation backing our networking abstraction layer
3. abstraction layer for platform networking interface
4. protocol unit serialization and deserialization layer

Platform networking interfaces The underlying implementations and their limitations must be understood before abstracting them can be attempted. Our platforms are divided into two categories: the Berkeley-influenced [15] platforms such as Linux, Windows and Mac OS X in one category and Symbian in the other.

Symbian uses active objects to provide an asynchronous interface to normal socket operations. The major difference to the normal Berkeley-style interface is the fact that Symbian sockets do not support synchronous operation at all.

Platform-specific implementations The differences within the Berkeley category are subtle enough so that grouping them under a single implementation is feasible and painless.

The relevant differences we encountered between the UNIX implementations and the Windows implementations can be seen from Table 4. All of these problems could be circumvented by simple cpp macros and a typedef.

Table 4. UNIX and Windows socket differences

	UNIX	Windows
initialization	*none*	WSAStartup()
error query	myerr = errno	myerr = WSAGetLastError()
errno values	EINPROGRESS / EAGAIN	WSAEWOULDBLOCK / WSAEWOULDBLOCK
ioctl call	ioctl()	ioctlsocket()
shutdown() arguments	SHUT_RDWR	SD_BOTH
sockaddr length type	socklen_t	*none*

The Symbian implementation is completely disjoint from the Berkeley-family implementation. It uses its own data structures, descriptor buffers and active objects to interface with the Symbian platform networking interface. Conversion from descriptor buffers to buffers in machine-independent code (**char** *) and vice versa is currently inefficiently done using memory copy.

Abstraction layer As noted above, the only major difference between the two families of platform network interfaces is Symbian's inability to do synchronous operation. This is not a hindrance at all, since being a single-threaded application, asynchronous network operation is the only choice if we do not want to block the entire UI in case of e.g. network congestion.

For managing connections, we need two different interface functions: one for initiating a connection and one for disconnecting. The asynchronous nature of the TCP connection is handled internally. In case the connection to the server is not successful, the situation is no different from the user perspective as a

Table 5. Machine Independent Networking Interface

```
int              network_init(struct network *net);
void             network_exit(struct network *net);

int              network_enqueue(struct network *net, uint8_t *data,
                                 size_t datalen, int message_type);
struct netbuf *  network_dequeue(struct network *net);
void             network_buf_done(struct netbuf *buf);

int              network_connect(struct network *net,
                                 const char *address,
                                 unsigned short port);
void             network_disconnect(struct network *net);
```

failed login and it will be treated as such: the network functionality will be unavailable to the user.

Network send and receive functions in a two-level fashion. Sending data onto the network first puts the data onto a network buffer list. This is done synchronously from the application point-of-view. We cannot directly always attempt to send data onto the network, since the network might be congested, the socket buffer therefore full, and sending would either block or fail, depending on if we were operating in blocking or non-blocking mode [15]. After data has entered the network buffer list, it is periodically drained onto the network using the GLUT timer functionality. Receiving data happens conversely: the network buffer queue is periodically filled by a function called from a GLUT timer handler and the application can read complete protocol data units off it synchronously.

To reduce the strain on memory allocation for the clients, this layer is not completely protocol-agnostic, but knows also about the application protocol framing mechanism we use, so that it can allocate memory chunks of the correct size for incoming transmissions.

Protocol serialization layer To avoid subtle but difficultly trackable incompatibility issues between the various client platforms and the server, the from- and to-wire routines are autogenerated from an XML representation.

The interface used to access the protocol unit contents is simply struct member access provided by the C language. A single PDU is always represented by a single structure and the structure representation is auto generated from the XML information. After all fields have been filled, the autogenerated serialize() routine is called to produce a byte stream representation of the contents of the structure. Conversely, deserialize() is called for a byte stream received from the network to fill out a struct representation of the same byte stream.

4 Conclusions and future work

Writing a portable mobile application for UNIX, Windows 98/2000/XP and Windows CE is simple when compared to the situation with Symbian. Symbian is a different type of system and many normal programming idioms were found to be unsuitable for Symbian. However, including Symbian produces a symbiotic relationship between the platforms: the requirements of Symbian keeps questionable programming practices down to a minimum while tools available on other platforms aid development on Symbian.

The scheduling model used by Symbian causes major problems: most platform functionality is a schedulable service, which in turn causes its interface to be asynchronous. For software with prior design elements based on synchronous interfaces, we showed an acceptable method for emulating synchronous interfaces on Symbian. Another major set of differences are memory limitations, both the lack of a read/write data segment on Symbian as well as the small amounts of main memory and lack of secondary memory on PDA/mobile devices.

When attempting to write software with code portability to multiple platforms, it is most important to understand the limitations and characteristics of each platform and make design decisions based upon that understanding. If platform expertise is not available at the beginning of the project, resources for some necessary development iteration to get the interfaces right should be allocated. The main goal is to make, as far as reasonably possible, all components either shared or behave similarly on all platforms. This will not only unify the user experience across various platforms, but, more importantly, reduce development, maintenance and testing effort.

Future work with the project includes unifying the user interface and program menu code: currently Symbian uses its native components while other platforms use OpenGL. In addition, unifying the build system to support a single project file across all our platforms needs work.

References

[1] Matti Dahlbom. Image loading and color reduction. 2003. URL http://www.newlc.com/Image-loading-and-color-reduction.html.

[2] Pantrazio de Mauro. Internationalizing messages in linux programs. *Linux Journal*, 1999(March 1999).

[3] Richard Harrison. *Symbian OS C++ for Mobile Phones*. Wiley, 2003.

[4] Martin Husemann. Fighting the lemmings. In *EuroBSDCon*, pages 45–53, 2004.

[5] Steve Johnson and Dennis Ritchie. Portability of C programs and the UNIX system. *The Bell System Technical Journal*, 57(6):2021–2048, June–August 1978.

[6] Mark J. Kilgard. *The OpenGL Utility Toolkit (GLUT) Programming Interface API Version 3*. 1996.

[7] David G. Korn. Porting UNIX to Windows NT. In *USENIX Annual Technical Conference*, pages 43–57, 1997.

[8] Paul Kunz. Building with automake.

[9] Jackie Neider, Tom Davis, and Mason Woo. *OpenGL Programming Guide*. Addison-Wesley Publishing Company, 1993.

[10] Nicholas Nethercote and Julian Seward. Valgrind: A program supervision framework. *Electronic Notes in Theoretical Computer Science*, 89(2), 2003.

[11] Geoffrey J. Noer. Cygwin32: A free Win32 porting layer for UNIX applications. In *2nd USENIX Windows NT Symposium*, 1998.

[12] Nokia Corporation. Symbian OS: Active objects and the active scheduler. 2004.

[13] Antti Nurminen and Ville Helin. Technical challenges in mobile real-time 3D city maps with dynamic content. In *IAESTED Software Engineering*, 2005.

[14] Niels Provos, Markus Friedl, and Peter Honeyman. Preventing privilege escalation. In *12th USENIX Security Symposium*, pages 231–241, 2003.

[15] W. Richard Stevens. *UNIX Network Programming*, volume 1. 1998.

[16] Symbian. Symbian developer library, 2003. URL `http://www.symbian.com/developer/techlib/v70sdocs/doc\_source/reference/cpp/AsynchronousServices/CActiveSchedulerClass.html`.

[17] Martin Tasker. *Professional Symbian programming*. Wrox Press, 2000.

[18] Paul Todd. Finding initialized or uninitialized static data in a dll. 2004.

[19] Uresh Vahalia. *UNIX Internals: The New Frontiers*. Prentice Hall, 1996.

[20] Robbert van Renesse. Goal-oriented programming, or composition using events, or threads considered harmful. In *ACM SIGOPS European Workshop*, pages 82–87, 1998.

[21] Peter van Sebille. EMame: a MAME port to EPOC Release 5 and Symbian platform v 6.0. 2001.

Adapting Aspect-Oriented Applications: A Trial Experience

Claudia Marcos and Jane Pryor

E-mail: {cmarcos,jpryor}@exa.unicen.edu.ar
ISISTAN Research Institute, Facultad de Ciencias Exactas, UNICEN
Paraje Arroyo Seco, B7001BBO Tandil, Argentina
Tel/Fax: + 54–2293–440362/3 http://www.exa.unicen.edu.ar/~isistan/

Abstract. During a system's life cycle, new requirements or changes in the existing ones imply modifying the system. Aspect-oriented software development is a new approach to the modularization of systems, yet it does not provide mechanisms to aid the evolution of software. The effort required to support the evolution greatly depends on the tool used for its construction. For this reason, the selection of a tool should also take into account its support for implementing evolving requirements. In this paper we present a comparison of two different tools, AspectJ and Alpheus, to support the construction and evolution of aspect-oriented applications. AspectJ is an aspect-oriented programming language based on Java. Alpheus is an aspect-oriented development tool based on a reflective framework.

Keyword. System evolution, unanticipated system evolution, aspect-oriented applications, aosd evolution, reflective architecture for aspects.

1 Introduction

All systems evolve during their life cycle due to new requirements or to changes in their functionality [1]. A system's evolution may be anticipated or unanticipated in its development. When the evolution has been anticipated, the changes to a system can be carried out without major problems. However, unanticipated evolution usually produces deterioration of a system. For this reason it is very important to have tools which support unanticipated system evolution.

The aspect-oriented paradigm provides constructors which encapsulate the elements whose code tends to be disseminated throughout many functional components. These constructors are called *aspects* [2] [3]. The goals of this paradigm are the encapsulation of these aspects and the minimization of the

Please use the following format when citing this chapter:

Marcos, C., Pryor, J., 2006, in IFIP International Federation for Information Processing, Volume 219, Advanced Software Engineering: Expanding the Frontiers of Software Technology, eds. Ochoa, S., Roman, G.-C., (Boston: Springer), pp. 153–161.

dependency among them and the basic functional components. In general terms, the system qualities obtained through the separation of concerns also have an impact on the ease of a system's evolution, due to independent and well encapsulated code.

This work presents an evaluation and documentation of different techniques, tools and programming languages, for the development and evolution of aspect-oriented software. In order to carry out this evaluation, a case study was developed. To study the impact of evolution, requirements were modified and also added at different stages of the life cycle, using these tools. The example was developed with AspectJ, a language for aspect-oriented programming, and with Alpheus, a visual tool for the construction of aspect-oriented applications. Then it is evaluated how the tools supported changes in requirements, both during the development of the application and once completed, and the incorporation of new requirements.

The following two sections introduce AspectJ and Alpheus, respectively. Section 4 describes the example used to compare both tools. Section 5 shows how the example is developed with Alpheus, and how it supports the system's evolution and the evaluation of this support. In Section 6 the example and evaluation is developed using AspectJ. The remaining section presents the conclusions.

2. AspectJ: an Aspect-Oriented Programming Language

AspectJ extends Java with new kind of classes called *aspects* [2]. These aspects crosscut the classes, interfaces and other aspects. In AspectJ, an aspect is a Java class, but it adds five new entities: join-points, point-cuts, introductions, advices and aspects themselves.

A *join-point* is a well-defined point in the execution of a program, such as method calls, method executions, access to attributes, exception handling, etc. A *point-cut* captures a collection of events in the program execution. It is a structure which has been designed to identify and select join-points in an AspectJ program. When a join-point is reached in the primary application code, the corresponding point-cut is activated and the aspect code is executed. The *advices* define the implementation code of the aspect, which is to be executed in the places defined by the point-cuts. *Introductions* and *declarations* are used to change the original structure of a program by adding or extending interfaces and classes. They may introduce new elements such as methods, constructors, or attributes.

3. Alpheus: A Tool for Aspect-Oriented Applications

Alpheus is a tool based on a reflective framework [4] that supports the development of aspect-oriented applications of different domains, enhancing desired software qualities such as adaptability and reuse [5][6]. The support for aspects that Alpheus provides has the following characteristics:

- **Flexible strategies for the runtime association and activation of aspects**: that is at what point the thread of control to the aspect [7]. When all methods and objects of a specified class are associated to an aspect: we call this strategy *class association*. When some methods are associated to an aspect: *method association*. When some objects are associated to an aspect: *object association*. When a particular method of an object is associated to an aspect: *object-method association*. Additionally, the activation of the aspect can take place *before* and/or *after* the intercepted method.

- **Reuse of planes**: The concept of *planes* has been introduced in order to obtain a clear separation and encapsulation of concerns. A *plane* is a collection of aspects which carry out similar or related functionality.
- **Definition and solving of conflicts between competing aspects**: *Conflicts* may occur if two or more aspects compete for activation. Different categories of conflict activation policies and different levels of granularity between conflicts are defined [6].

The tool allows developers to define the components of the application and then generates the Java code of the application. Alpheus also provides the visualization of the components of an application, plus some UML diagrams [8].

4 An Example – Personal Web Server

A Personal Web Server (PWS) is a server application which receives petitions for documents from a web client, locates and then sends the document. The HyperText Transfer Protocol (HTTP) is used to establish the connection. HTTP is a simple protocol implemented in TCP/IP. The HTTP client sends a document identifier to the server and the server replies by sending HTML documents or common text. A firewall is a filter mechanism that applies security policies to the network traffic. The firewall has some access policies applied from and to the external network.

This example will evolve in two different ways. During its development, the new requirement is the necessity to register the access of the HTML documents stored in the PWS. When it is working it is necessary to store other types of documents (gif, jpg) not only HTML. It is also necessary to introduce a new firewall at night time for some statistics.

As the PWS has a server which offers services to clients, the natural architecture for this system is a client-server one [9]. Clients have to know which servers are available but they do not know anything about the other clients [1].

5. Personal Web Server with Alpheus

Three planes are defined in Alpheus: *PlanoFirewall*, containing the policies related to the access from and to the network; *PlanoIncidencias*, containing the actions log; and *Base*, containing the functional application. The aspects and objects are then defined for each plane.

The composition (called association) between the aspects and objects can be defined. For each association it is necessary to specify when and how the aspect is activated (before, after, etc.), plus the strategy to follow (class, method, class-method, etc). For the PWS two associations have been defined.

The first association is in order to control the access to the network. It is defined between the OFirewall object and the ASP_Firewall aspect of the PlanoFirewall plane. The association has some characteristics: *before*, because the aspect is to be activated before the base element; *method-reflection*, as the reglas_red(id) method of the OFirewall class will be modified by the aspect's functionality. The second association is created to store the access to the HTML documents. It is defined between the MC_Firewall aspect of the PlanoFirewall plane and the ASP_Incidences of the PlanoIncidencias plane.

6.2.1 Evolution during Development

A new requirement is introduced the access to HTML documents is to be registered by the system because statistics. In order to support this new requirement a new plane is defined, *PlanoEstadistica*. Secondly, the aspects in this plane are specified (ASP_Estadistica) (Figure 2). Lastly, an association is established between the OConnectionThread of the base plane and the newly created ASP_Estadistica of the PlanoEstadistica plane. As a result, whenever the OConnectionThread is invoked the ASP_Estadistica oversees the access to the HTML documents.

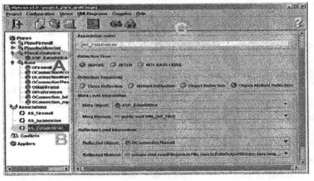

Figure 2. Evolution during development

6.2.2 Evolution When the System is Working

Once the system components were defined Alpheus uses this specification of the application and generates the corresponding Java code. Once the system is working, it is necessary to register the access to all documents, not only HTML. To support this, the add_statistic method of the ASP_Estadistica aspect has to be modified and the aspect has to be recompiled.

The system continues to evolve when it is necessary to introduce a new firewall for night-time. The new plane PlanoFirewallNoche and the aspect ASP_Firewall_noche are specified (Figure 4). The association between the Firewall class of the base plane and the ASP_Firewall_noche aspect is specified.

This new composition causes a conflict between aspects, because when an OFirewall object receives a message, two aspects compete for activation:

ASP_Firewall and ASP_Firewall_noche. The activation of the firewalls depends on the time of day, therefore it is not possible to determine before-hand which of the aspects has to be activated (context-dependent conflict). To solve this type of conflict, the designer specifies the conflict and the programmer inserts the corresponding code. For the rest of conflicts the tool generates automatically the solution.

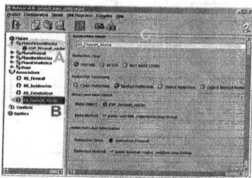

Figure 4. FirewallNoche association

6.3 Personal Web Server with AspectJ

The PWS application was also developed with Java (IDE) Borland JBuilder6 Enterprise and AspectJ. For the PWS example, two aspects have to be coded. The ASP_Firewall aspect (Figure 5 A) implements the policies of the firewall, crosscutting the Firewall class as it is in charge of supervising the access to the HTML document. The second aspect is called ASP_Incidences, and it registers the events of the application by storing them in a data base.

The ASP_Firewall aspect defines a point-cut for the invocation of the reglas_red method of the Firewall class (Figure 5 B). The advice (Figure 5 C) has been declared as *before*. Before analyzing whether the access to the document is allowed, the ASP_Firewall modifies the result variable of the firewall object according to the information retrieved from the database.

```
package webserver;
import webserver.Firewall;

aspect ASP_Firewall
{
    declare dominates: ASP_Firewall,ASP_Estadisticas;
    connection_bd bd;

    public ASP_Firewall()
    {
        bd = new connection_mysql();           A
        bd.connection();
    }                                                    B

    public pointcut acceso(Firewall firewall):
        execution(boolean Firewall.reglas_red(String))&&this(firewall);

    before(Firewall firewall): acceso(firewall)
    {
        string ip = firewall.getip();              C
        firewall.set_result(acceso(ip));
    }

    public boolean access(String ip)
    {
        return bd.reglas_red(ip);
    }
}
```

Figure 5. Aspect definition with AspectJ

The application code is generated in two steps: firstly the weaver converts the aspect code to Java code, and secondly, the Java compiler generates the Java object code (.class), where the application and aspect code are mixed together.

6.3.1 Evolution During Development

Because AspectJ is a programming language and is therefore used during the implementation phase, it is not really possible to evaluate evolution during development. However, it is possible to introduce the new requirement by creating a new aspect called ASP_Estadistica (Figure 6). This aspect will register the access to the HTML documents when the sendFile of the ConnectionThread class is invoked. Section A of Figure 6 describes the definition of the aspect, and section B shows the point-cut and its *estadistica* advice.

The joint point for the point-cut *estadistica* is related to the sendFile method of the ConnectionThread class and the ct instance. This aspect registers the access to the HTML documents in the system database.

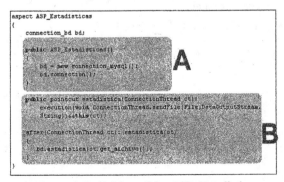

Figure 6. Definition of the ASP_Estadisticas aspect

6.3.2 Evolution When the System is Working

Once the system is working it is necessary to register the access to all kinds of documents and not only the HTML ones. The system is then extended in order to introduce a new firewall for night-time analysis, so the ASP_FirewallNoche is added. The ASP_FirewallNoche aspect is activated when the documents are requested from 00:00 hrs to 8:00 hrs. To support the activation of the aspect during the night a conditional sentence has to be implemented. The ASP_Firewall aspect also has to be modified introducing the conditional sentence to decide when this aspect has to be activated (during the day).

The ASP_Firewall and ASP_FirewallNoche aspects have a conflictive situation which is not of precedence but dependent on the context, because their activation depends on the time. AspectJ does not support this kind of conflict so the solution has to be coded into the aspects. The only mechanism supported by AspectJ for the resolution of conflicts is of precedence. Both aspects have to be modified in order to introduce the sentences needed to verify the hour.

3. Comparison of the Tools

These tools were evaluated in their support for the system evolution in two ways: their flexibility to support changes in the requirements, and their extensibility for introducing new functionality. Moreover, they also were evaluated during the system development and once the system is working.

As Alpheus is a research tool it is free and open-source (http://www.exa.unicen.edu.ar/catedras/reflex/). The available documentation may be found in the form of papers describing Alpheus, the reflective framework it instantiates, and how it works by means of examples. The user interface of Alpheus is very intuitive and friendly. To aid the designer, Alpheus also provides consistency validation and visualization of the application by means of different diagrams and also provides some UML diagrams.

AspectJ provides the means to code aspect-oriented applications using a well-known development environment. Java developers therefore have all the support necessary to begin with the development of aspect-oriented applications. AspectJ does not support the resolution of different kinds of conflicts that an application may have. AspectJ has very good documentation and it is widely-used for the development of aspect-oriented applications. The development environment used with AspectJ provides some extra benefits, such as code generation, different kinds of reports, code documentation, etc. Table 1 shows the results of the evaluation of the example evolution using AspectJ (AJ) and Alpheus (A).

Table 4. Tools Evaluation

Evolution	Statistics for HTML Documents		Statistics Extension		Night-time Firewall	
Elements to Evaluate	AJ	A	AJ	A	AJ	A
Viability of implementing new requirements	YES	YES	YES	YES	YES	YES
Number of classes to be implemented	0	0	0	0	0	0
Number of classes to be modified	0	1	0	1	0	1
Number of aspects to be created	1	1	1	0	1	1
Classes to be compiled	13	2	13	1	13	2
Implementation time	20 min	30 min	20 min	30 min	30 min	45 min

7 Conclusion

This paper presents an evaluation of two different tools, Alpheus and AspectJ, which support the development of aspect-oriented applications. They were evaluated analyzing their support for the evolution by the development of an example.

Alpheus is a visual development tool which instantiates a reflective framework. With this tool it is possible to specify all the components of an aspect-oriented application and then automatically generate the corresponding code. It also provides different levels of visualization of the application and automatic detection of conflicts. AspectJ is an aspect-oriented programming language based on Java which introduces some new concepts in order to code aspects and their characteristics.

One of the main differences in the tools is the way in which the aspect weaving process is carried out. In Alpheus, the weaving is done at run-time and AspectJ has a static weaver, but on the other hand, the performance is better. In both tools it was possible to support the evolution of the Personal Web Server application, and the amount of aspects and classes needed for this evolution were almost the same. In AspectJ it was always necessary to recompile all the classes and in Alpheus only the affected classes are compiled again.

8 Bibliography

[1] I. Sommerville. *Ingeniería de Software*. Sexta edición 2002.

[2] Aspect-Oriented Programming Home Page. At Http://aosd.net

[3] AOSD 2002, 1st. International Conference on Aspect-Oriented Software Development. Enschede. Gregor Kiczales, ed., (ACM Press, The Netherlands, 2002).

[4] P. Maes. Concepts and Experiments in Computational Reflection. In Proceedings of OOPSLA '87.

[5] J. Pryor, and C. Marcos. Constructing Aspect-Oriented Applications using a Reflective Framework. Technical Report TR-28-02, ISISTAN Research Institute, Universidad Nacional del Centro de la Provincia de Buenos Aires (UNICEN), 2002.
[6] F. Valentino, A. Ramos, C. Marcos, and J. Pryor, A Framework for the Development of Multi-Level Reflective Applications. Proc. of the Second Argentine Symposium on Software Engineering (ASSE), Argentina, 2001.
[7] C. Marcos, Patrones de Diseño como Entidades de Primera Clase, PhD. Thesis, Facultad de Ciencias Exactas, ISISTAN Research Institute, Universidad Nacional del Centro de la Provincia de Buenos Aires (UNICEN), April 2001.
[8] G. Booch, J. Rumbaugh, and I. Jacobson. *The Unified Modeling Language.* User Guide (Addison-Wesley, 1999).
[9] F. Buschmann, R. Meunier, H. Rohnert, P. Sommerlad, and M. Stal. *Pattern-Oriented Software Architecture - A System of Patterns.* John Wiley & Sons, 1996.

Building a 3D Meshing Framework Using Good Software Engineering Practices*

N. Hitschfeld, C. Lillo, A. Cáceres, M. C. Bastarrica, and M. C. Rivara

Computer Science Department, FCFM, Universidad de Chile
{nancy|clillo|acaceres|cecilia|mcrivara}@dcc.uchile.cl

Abstract. 3D meshing tools are complex pieces of software involving varied algorithms generally with high computing demands. New requirements and techniques appear continuously and being able to incorporate them into existing tools helps keep them up to date. Modifying complex software is generally a complex task and software engineering strategies such as object-orientation and design patterns promote modifiability and flexibility. We present the design of a 3D meshing framework based on these concepts that yields a software that is both flexible at runtime and easy to modify, while not sacrificing performance severely. We also present an evaluation of the framework design quality and performance.

1 Introduction

A mesh is a discretization of a domain geometry. It may be composed of triangles or quadrilaterals in 2D, or tetrahedra or hexahedra in 3D. Building 3D meshing tools is a challenging task involving diverse issues: (a) depending on the application field where the tools are used, different algorithms are more appropriate than others, so there is the option of having either a multiplicity of different tools or a flexible software that adapts to different contexts; (b) 3D meshing is a very active research area, where new approaches, criteria, and algorithms are proposed continuously; if a tool is to have a long life, it should be able to incorporate these changes without much effort; and (c) tools should be able to manage big meshes, so performance issues such as efficient processing and storage usage are relevant and should be taken into account.

Mesh generation tools have usually been developed by their final users, i.e. mathematicians, physicists or engineers. This caused that not always the best methods for software development have been applied. We believe that there is an opportunity to improve the quality of meshing tools by applying the best software engineering practices known.

---

*The work of N. Hitschfeld, A. Cáceres and C. Lillo was supported by Fondecyt N°1030672. The work of M. C. Rivara was supported by Fondecyt N°1040713.

Please use the following format when citing this chapter:

Hitschfeld, N., Lillo, C., Cáceres, A., Bastarrica, M.C., Rivara, M.C., 2006, in IFIP International Federation for Information Processing, Volume 219, Advanced Software Engineering: Expanding the Frontiers of Software Technology, eds. Ochoa, S., Roman, G.-C., (Boston: Springer), pp. 162–170.

1.1 Good Practices in Software Engineering

The main goal of software engineering is to develop good practices so that to obtain good software. The are qualities related to software execution such as correctness and performance, that are well understood. However, there is another set of qualities that have been gaining relevance lately: flexibility, reusability or modifiability. These qualities are relevant because the cost of modifying software is high. Algorithms and data structures have a determinant influence over performance. Similarly, software design techniques such as object-orientation, design patterns or software architecture have more influence over the attributes not related to execution. Reaching the desired software quality depends on the requirements at hand. Generally optimizing some attributes can only be done at the expense of other qualities. Sophisticated meshing tools implementing high performing algorithms and data structures are usually less reusable, and certainly less maintainable. So a compromise among the required attributes is generally the best solution.

Software reuse promotes productivity and high quality. Software already developed can be incorporated in new systems saving development time and costs, and also counting on the properties of the reused parts. One of the known efforts to make available robust, efficient, flexible and easy to use implementations of geometric algorithms and data structures is the reusable library CGAL [5]. Software families is a modern approach based on planned massive reuse. A product family is a set of products that are built from a collection of reused assets in a planned manner. There have been some attempts in using software product family concepts for building meshing tools [2, 4].

1.2 3D Tetrahedral Meshing Tools

Meshing tools allow us to solve partial differential equations numerically or to visualize objects. In 3D, different meshing tools vary in the type of the elements they manage; the most widely used are tetrahedral and hexahedral meshes. There are several 3D tetrahedral meshing tools currently available but not all of them provide the same functionality [9] varying depending on the application for which they were designed.

Three examples of known meshing tools are TetGen, TetMesh and QMG. TetGen [13] is a very efficient and robust open source tool for the generation of quality Delaunay meshes for solving partial differential equations using finite element and finite volume methods. TetGen has been developed using C++, but not necessarily object-oriented concepts, since it is implemented using a few classes and without using inheritance, polymorphism, information hiding or encapsulation. TetMesh [7] is a commercial product for the generation of quality tetrahedral meshes for finite element methods. It was originally developed in FORTRAN 77 and afterwards migrated to C. QMG [8] is an open source octree based mesh generator for automatic unstructured finite element mesh generation. It was developed in C++ and Tcl/tk using object-orientation concepts, but since it uses octrees as the main data structure, all algorithms should conform to this structure, yielding an efficient yet highly coupled tool. In general, all the mesh generation tools are focused on reaching efficiency and robustness and not extensibility and modifiability.

1.3 Our Meshing Framework

The motivation of our work is to design and develop a framework that allows us the construction of new 3D meshing tools with little effort. We would like to have the flexibility of easily interchanging or adding new input/output data formats, mesh generation algorithms for each step, quality criteria and refinement/improvement region shapes. We have already designed the architecture of a family of 2D meshing tools [2] and now we have extended it for the generation of 3D mesh generators. The framework is implemented in C++ and currently includes Delaunay and Lepp-based algorithms, among others.

In this paper we propose a 3D tetrahedral meshing framework whose design is based on object-orientation and design patterns in order to achieve the flexibility and evolvability required, without sensibly sacrificing performance.

2 Framework Analysis, Design and Implementation

The framework has been developed using object-orientation and design patterns. Functional requirements were specified using UML use-case diagrams and described with sequence diagrams. Software structure was specified using class diagrams [2].

2.1 Requirements and Analysis

A flexible and complete 3D mesh generation framework should implement each one of the following processes:

- input geometry in different formats;
- generation of an initial volume mesh that fits the domain geometry;
- refinement/improvement of a mesh in order to satisfy the quality criteria;
- smoothing of the mesh according to a certain smoothing parameter;
- derefinement of a mesh according to density requirements;
- quality evaluation of the generated mesh;
- visualization of the mesh.

The specification of the input geometry and physical values can be generated by CAD programs or by other mesh generation tools. We have already

---

[2]Part of the framework design documentation can be found in http://www.dcc.uchile.cl/~nancy/framework/diagrams.html.

implemented the Off and Mesh formats. The algorithms that generate the initial volume mesh can receive as input the domain geometry described as a triangulated surface mesh or as a general polyhedron. We have implemented an initial volume mesh that fulfills the Delaunay condition and an initial volume tetrahedralization that may not satisfy it.

The initial volume mesh is the input of the refinement step that divides coarse tetrahedra into smaller ones until the refinement criteria are fulfilled in the indicated region. Either the initial volume mesh or the refined mesh can be the input of the improvement process. The user must specify an improvement criterion and a region where the improvement is to be applied. At the moment, we have implemented the refinement and improvement strategies based on the Lepp-concept [10] but it is possible to add other strategies, such as the Delaunay refinement [11], without much effort. The smoothing and derefinement processes are also applied according to a criterion and over a region of the domain.

Once a mesh has been processed, the user has the possibility of evaluating its quality according to different criteria. This is useful if the user wants to see the distribution and percentage of good and bad elements in the mesh. The visualization process is currently done using Geomview [1]. Each mesh generation process can also be skiped by representing it with a dummy algorithm.

2.2 Design and Implementation

Figure 1 shows the most important part of the meshing framework class diagram. We represent each mesh generation process as an abstract class and each different strategy implementing each process as a concrete subclass. For example, the *Refine* abstract class is realized by subclasses LeppAlgorithms and VoronoiRefinement, as shown in Fig. 2. We also represent all the criteria with the *Criterion* abstract class and all the region shapes with the *Region* abstract class in Fig. 1. This allows a programmer to add a new criterion, region shape or strategy by adding just a concrete class that inherits from the respective abstract class and without modifying the source code. The code of a particular mesh generator uses the abstract classes code, and the user must select which concrete algorithms he/she wants to use for each mesh generation process, criteria and region shapes. For example, *Generate VolumeMesh* can be realized with GMVDelaunay to generate a Delaunay volume mesh. Similarly, the abstract class *Refine* can be realized with LeppAlgorithms receiving a *Region* and a *Criterion* as parameters realized as WholeGeometry and LongestEdge, respectively (see Fig. 2).

The mesh is modeled as a container object. The Mesh class provides methods for accessing and modifying its constituent elements (tetrahedra, faces, edges and points). Tetrahedron, Face, Edge and Vertex are also classes, each of them providing concrete functionality and also providing access to the neighborhood information. The mesh quality evaluation is modeled using the Evaluate class. This class uses a criterion and, according to some user parameters, it classifies the elements and generates a file with the evaluation results as output.

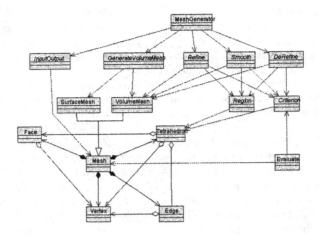

Fig. 1. Framework general class diagram

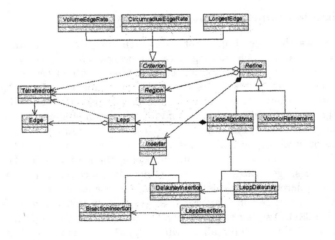

Fig. 2. Partial detailed class diagram

In the framework implementation, we used several design patterns [6]. Each different mesh generation process and each criterion follows the Strategy pattern. The region shape follows the Composite pattern. The mesh evaluation class follows the Observer pattern where the observed object is the Mesh. The interface is organized using the Command pattern. The mesh is a Singleton.

3 3D Framework Evaluation

Our goals was to achieve flexibility, modifiability and performance. While the first two depend on a good design, the last can only be evaluated at runtime.

3.1 Design Evaluation

Metrics for object-oriented design provide quantitative mechanisms for estimating design quality. Good metrics evaluation shows a good design but it does not guarantee good software. However, bad metrics evaluation almost guarantees bad software results. In this work, we use the metrics proposed in [3] because they are widely used for measuring flexibility and extensibility. A brief description of each metric is included in Table 1 and Table 2 shows the results of applying the metrics to the framework class diagram.

Name	Description
Weighted Methods per Class (WMC)	Sum of all method's complexity within a class. The number of methods and their complexity indicate the effort required for implementing a class. The larger the number of methods the more complex the inheritance tree will be, and also the more specific a class becomes, limiting its reusability.
Depth of Inheritance Tree (DIT)	Maximum length between the node and the root in the inheritance tree. The deeper the class, the more probable the class inherits a lot of methods. A deep class hierarchy may imply a complex design.
Number of children (NOC)	As the number of children grows, the abstraction represented by a class becomes vague, and its reusability decreases.
Coupling Between Objects (CBO)	It is the number of collaborations between a class and the rest of the system. As this number grows, the class reusability decreases. High values also make modifications and testing harder.
Response for a Class (RFC)	It is the number of methods that may be potentially executed as a response to a message received by a class object. As this metric grows, testing the class becomes harder, and the class complexity also grows.
Lack of Cohesion in Methods (LCOM)	A high LCOM indicates that methods can be grouped in disjoin sets with respect to attributes, and form two or more classes with them.

Table 1. Design metrics

	WMC	DIT	NOC	CBO	RFC	LCOM
Minimum	1	0	0	0	1	0
Maximum	36	2	8	22	36	100
Medium	7.60	0.60	0.50	3.87	12.67	30.98
St. Deviation	7.11	0.66	1.43	4.18	7.87	36.73

Table 2. Tool design evaluation

The WMC metric shows a value within the normal scope for this kind of system. There are only two classes out of this scope: **Predicates** and **Tetrahedron**. The former reuses a library described in [12]. The latter class contains several methods required for the Delaunay algorithm, such as the sphere test; thus it can be divided into two different classes: one that includes basic concepts about tetrahedron, and another one extending the first one that contains specific methods for Delaunay implementation. The DIT metric is always small, showing a low design complexity. The same occurs with the NOC metric. Both metrics can grow when extending the design. The CBO metric value is normal for an application with this size (52 classes). The maximum value is achieved in the `MeshGenerator` class that references the classes implementing the main processes and classes holding the main parameters, such as criteria and regions; this class is only used when the system is operated using the command line, so it can be excluded from the analysis. For the RFC metric, the values are within the normal scope for all classes except for `Predicates` and `Tetrahedron` for the same reasons explained for WMC. Finally, the LCOM metric has high values; however, the highest values are only found in abstract classes: their methods have no code, so they do not access instance variables; thus, the metric has no effect.

3.2 Performance Evaluation

Performance evaluation in 3D meshing tools is mainly related to the time it takes to execute typical mesh processes. Figure 3 shows an example of a volume before and after applying the refinement process and Fig. 4 shows the time as a function of the number of refined tetrahedra.

Fig. 3. Refinement process example: 170 points and 441 tetrahedra (left), and 8,823 points and 45,518 tetrahedra (right)

In general terms, a generated meshing tool with the same functionality as TetGen is around two times slower with respect to refinement and improvement. This difference may be due to the fact that in TetGen all data structures are accessed directly, not using information hiding or encapsulation, and there is no dynamic binding. On the other hand, the mesh generated mesh tool uses all these concepts.

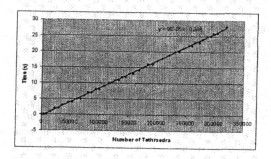

Fig. 4. Refinement framework time performance (executed in a Pentium IV processor with 2.6 GHZ and 1 GB RAM)

4 Conclusion

3D meshing tools are extremely complex software that apply resource consuming algorithms to big meshes. This is why performance has been the main focus of research around implementing this kind of software. However, since computers tend to have more and cheaper memory and CPU capacity, some of the burden has shifted towards the development process of the tools. In this context, we proposed an object-oriented design based on design patterns that has proved to yield a flexible and modifiable framework, without severely sacrificing performance.

References

1. Geometry Center at the University of Minnesota. Geomview, 1996. http://www.geomview.org.
2. M. C. Bastarrica and N. Hitschfeld-Kahler. Designing a Product Family of Meshing Tools. *Advances in Engineering Software*, 37(1):1–10, Jan 2006.
3. Shyan R. Chidamber and Chris F. Kemerer. A Metrics Suite for Object-Oriented Design. *IEEE Transactions on Software Engineering*, 20(6):476–493, June 1994.
4. A. H. ElSheikh, W. S. Smith, and S. E. Chidiac. Semi-formal design of reliable mesh generation systems. *Advances in Engineering Software*, 35(12):827–841, 2004.
5. Andrea Fabri. CGAL- the computational geometry algorithm library. In *Proceedings of the 10th Annual International Meshing Roundtable*, 2001.
6. Erich Gamma, Richard Helm, Ralph Hohnson, and Hohn Vlissides. *Design Patterns: Elements of Reusable Object Oriented Software*. Addison-Wesley, 1995.
7. Paul-Louis George, Frédéric Hecht, and Éric Saltel. TetMesh-GHS3D V3.1, the fast, reliable, high quality tetrahedral mesh generator and optimiser, 1986. White paper, http://www.simulog.fr/mesh/gener2.htm.

8. Scott A. Mitchell and Stephen A. Vavasis. Quality mesh generation in three dimensions. In *Proceedings of the Eighth Annual Symposium on Computational Geometry*, pages 212–221, Berlin, Germany, 1992. ACM.

9. Steve Owen. Meshing software survey, 1998. http://www.andrew.cmu.edu/user/sowen/softsurv.html.

10. María Cecilia Rivara. New Longest-Edge Algorithms for the Refinement and/or Improvement of Unstructured Triangulations. *International Journal for Numerical Methods in Engineering*, 40:3313–3324, 1997.

11. Jim Ruppert. A Delaunay Refinement Algorithm for Quality 2-Dimensional Mesh Generation. *Journal of Algorithms*, 18(3):548–585, May 1995.

12. J. Shewchuk. Adaptive Precision Floating-Point Arithmetic and Fast Robust Geometric Predicates. *Discrete & Comp. Geometry*, 18(3):305–363, 1997.

13. H. Si and K. Gärtner. Meshing Piecewise Linear Complexes by Constrained Delaunay Tetrahedralizations. In *Proc of the 14th International Meshing Roundtable*, 2005.